MEN AT WORK AND PLAY.

Original signed limited edition prints from many of
these photographs are available by writing to DMD
Photo Art at the address below:

DMD Photo Art
P.O. Box 104
Manchester M16 0PJ

First published in 1997.

The inclusion of photographs of any person in this
book should not be taken as any indication of their
views, attitudes or sexual orienation. All persons
depicted are over 18 years of age.

Book designed by Chris De Witt
(chrisx@dircon.co.uk)

ISBN 0 9530823 0 X

MEN AT WORK
AND PLAY

David Degare

INTRODUCTION

This book is not trying to make any kind of statement, but is just showing that after several years of photographing men in a documentary style I have always found them to be interesting, attractive, and above all fun to look at. The title is only a loose description for a wide range of subjects, but the men depicted are interesting because they are mainly shown just being themselves or at play.

I have only included a few written descriptions with the photographs because I think that the images speak for themselves, or better still they stimulate your imagination. Indeed I often have no idea who my subjects are, or anything about them (not even their telephone numbers!).

Most of the photographs were taken around Manchester and London and I thank everyone who has given me permission to print their picture.

VORWORT

Dieses Buch will keine Behauptung machen. Es zeigt aber, daß nach einigen Jahren, in den ich Männer im Dokumtarstil photographiert habe, finde ich sie immer interessant, anziehend und vor allem viel Spaß anzusehen. Der Titel ist nur eine freie Beschreibung einer großen Auswahl von Männern, aber diese dargestellte Männer sind interessant, weil sie sich hauptsächlich ganz natürlich zeigen, bei der Arbeit oder beim Spiel.

Ich habe nur ein paar geschriebener Schilderungen mit den Photos eingeschlossen, weil ich glaube, daß die Blider für sich sprechen, oder noch besser, die Phantasie stimulieren. Tatsächlich habe ich oft keine Idee, wer die Männer sind, und weiß auch nichts über sie (nicht einmal ihre Telefonnummern!).

Die meisten Photos wurden um Manchester und London gemacht, und ich danke ein jedem, der mir erlaubt hat, sein Bild zu veröffentlichen.

AVANT-PROPOS

Ce livre ne cherche pas à faire aucune déclaration, mais il fait voir qu'après avoir photographié les hommes dans une style documentaire pendant plusieurs années, je les trouve toujours intéressants, attrayants et surtout amusants à regarder. Le titre n'est qu'une description imprécise d'un grand choix de sujets, mais les hommes représentés sont intéressants en ce sens que la plupart se laissent voir au naturel, en travaillant ou en s'amusant.

Je n'ai inclus que quelques exposés écrit avec les photos, car je crois que les images parlent d'elles-mêmes, ou encore mieux, qu'elles excitent l'imagination. En effet, j'ai souvent aucune idée de qui sont mes sujets, et je ne sais rien d'eux (même pas leurs numéros de téléphone!).

La meilleure partie des photos ont été prises de ci de là à Manchester et à Londres, et je remercie chacun qui m'a permis d'imprimer son image.

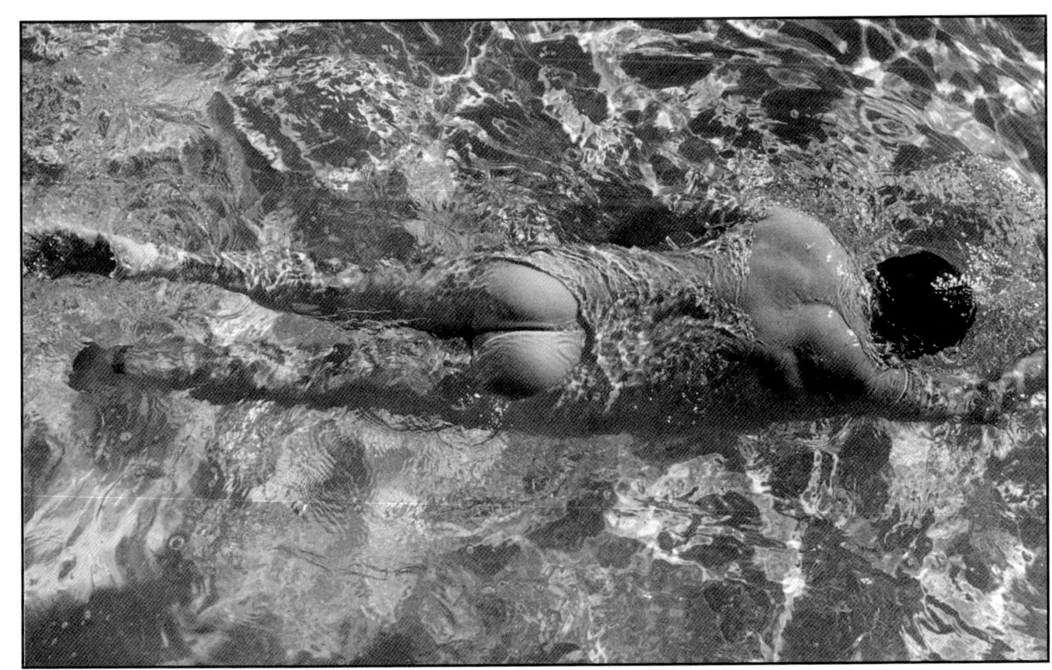

David Degare

TO ANDREW O'DONNEL

Many thanks to Andy, Chris, George and Oliver whithout whose help and encouragement this book would not have been possible.

LONDON GAY PRIDE AND MANCHESTER MARDI GRAS.

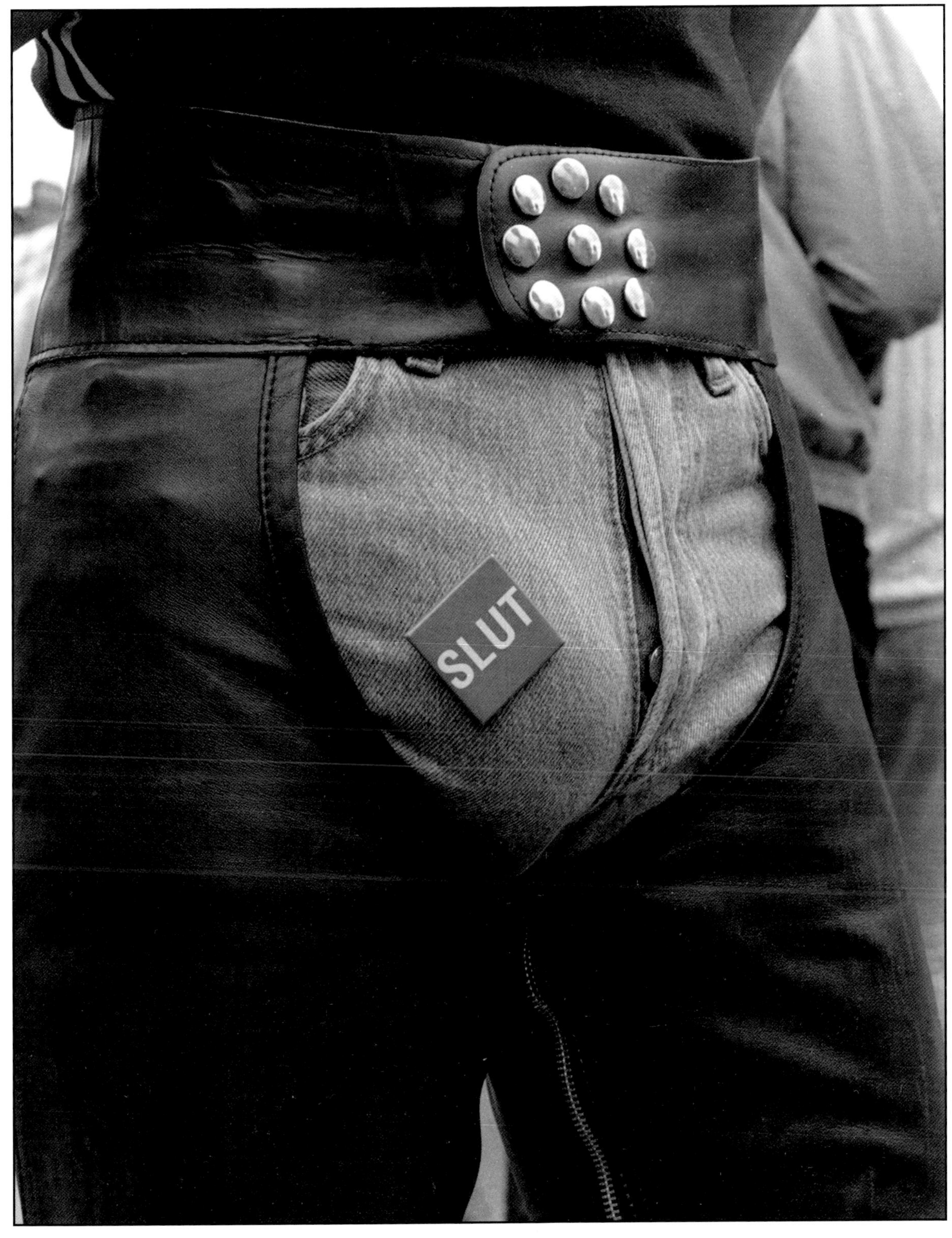
SLUT

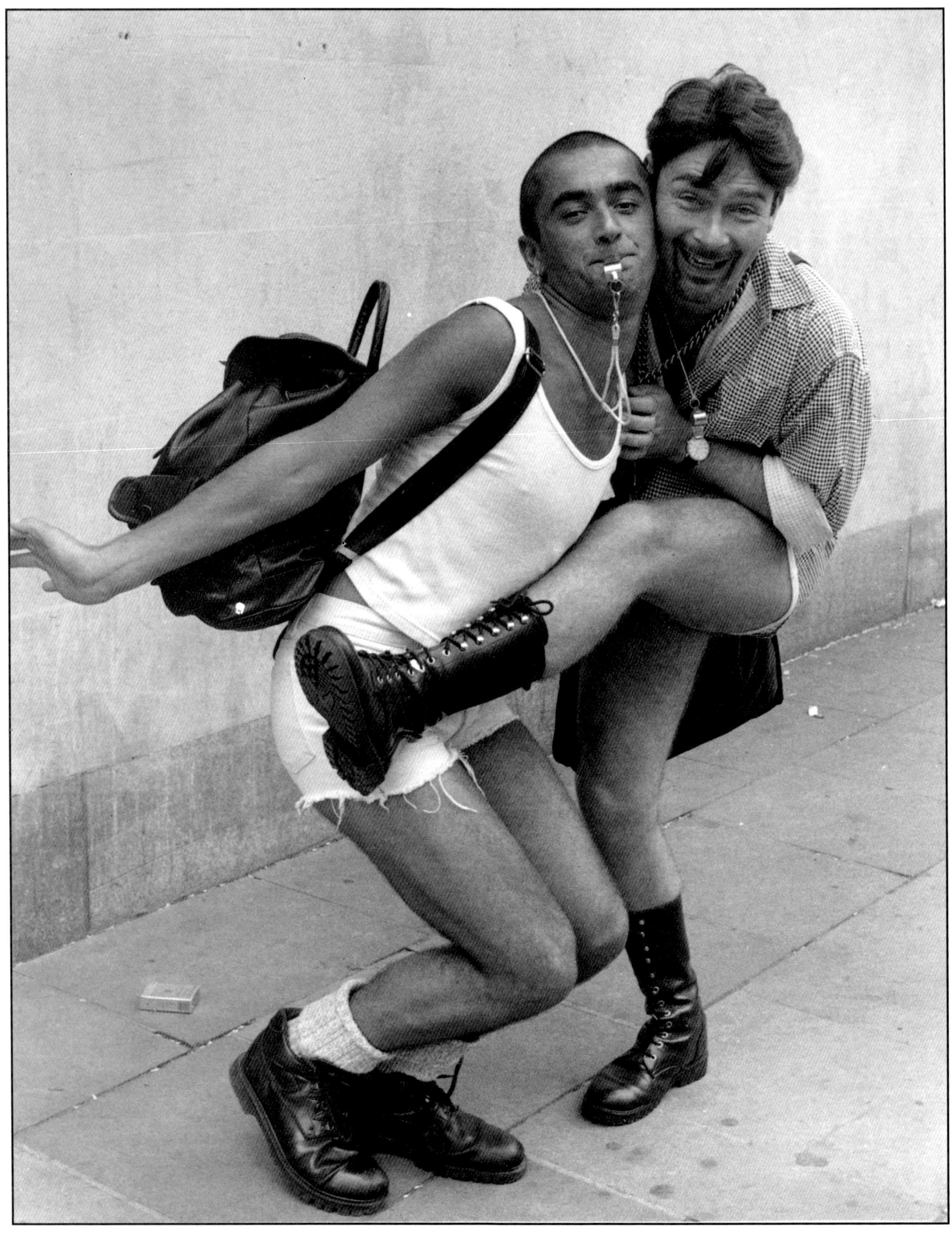

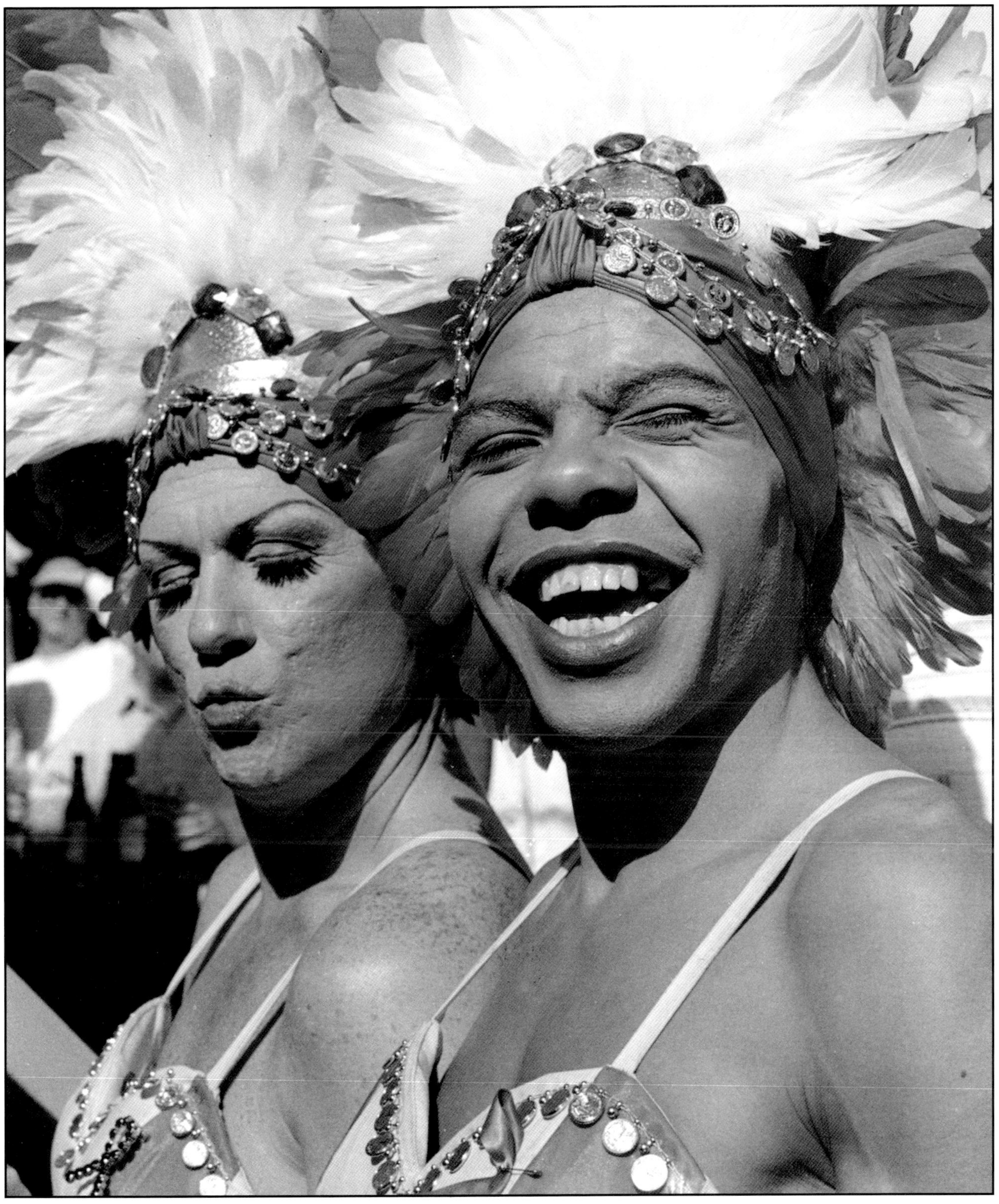

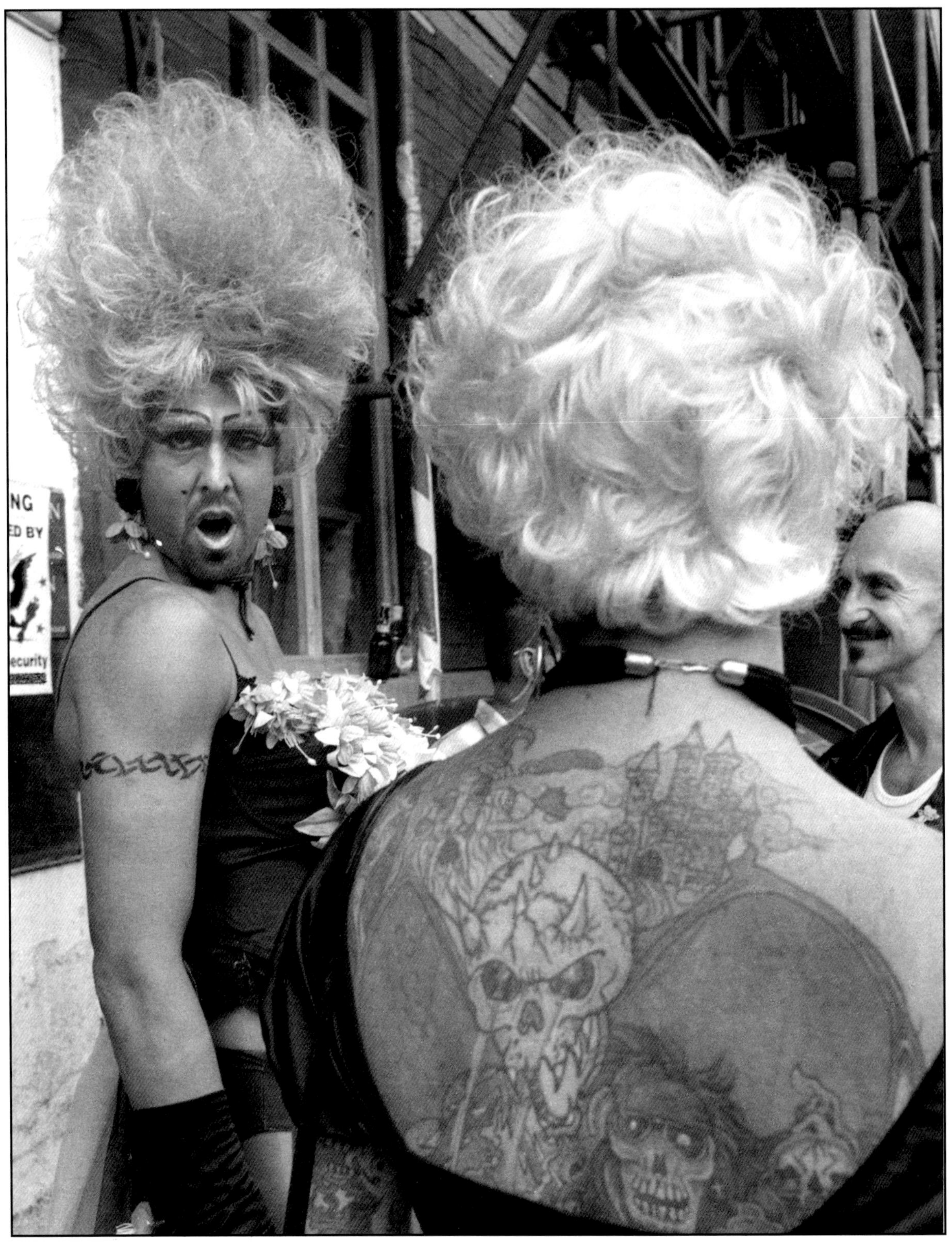
NG
ED BY
ecurity

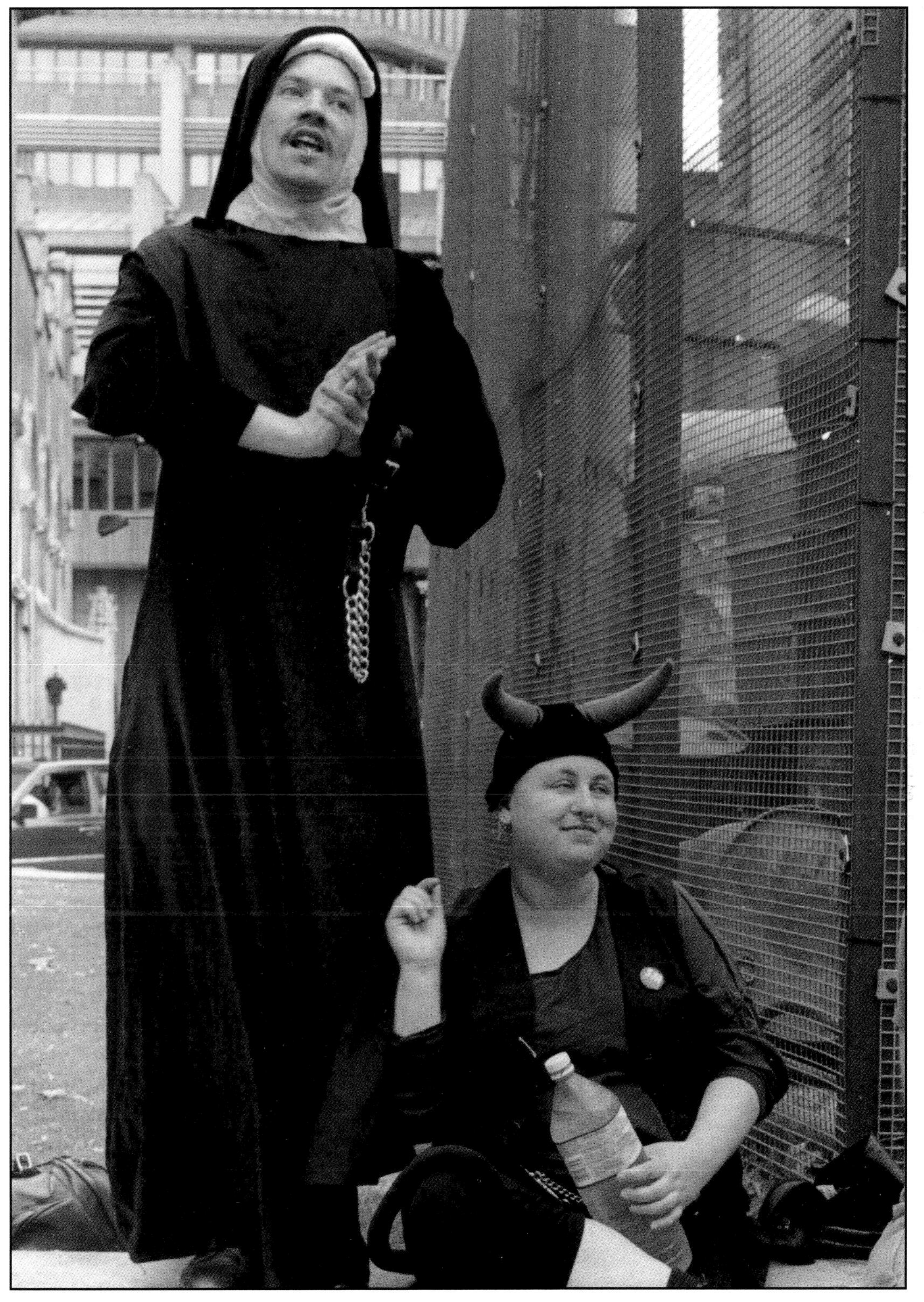

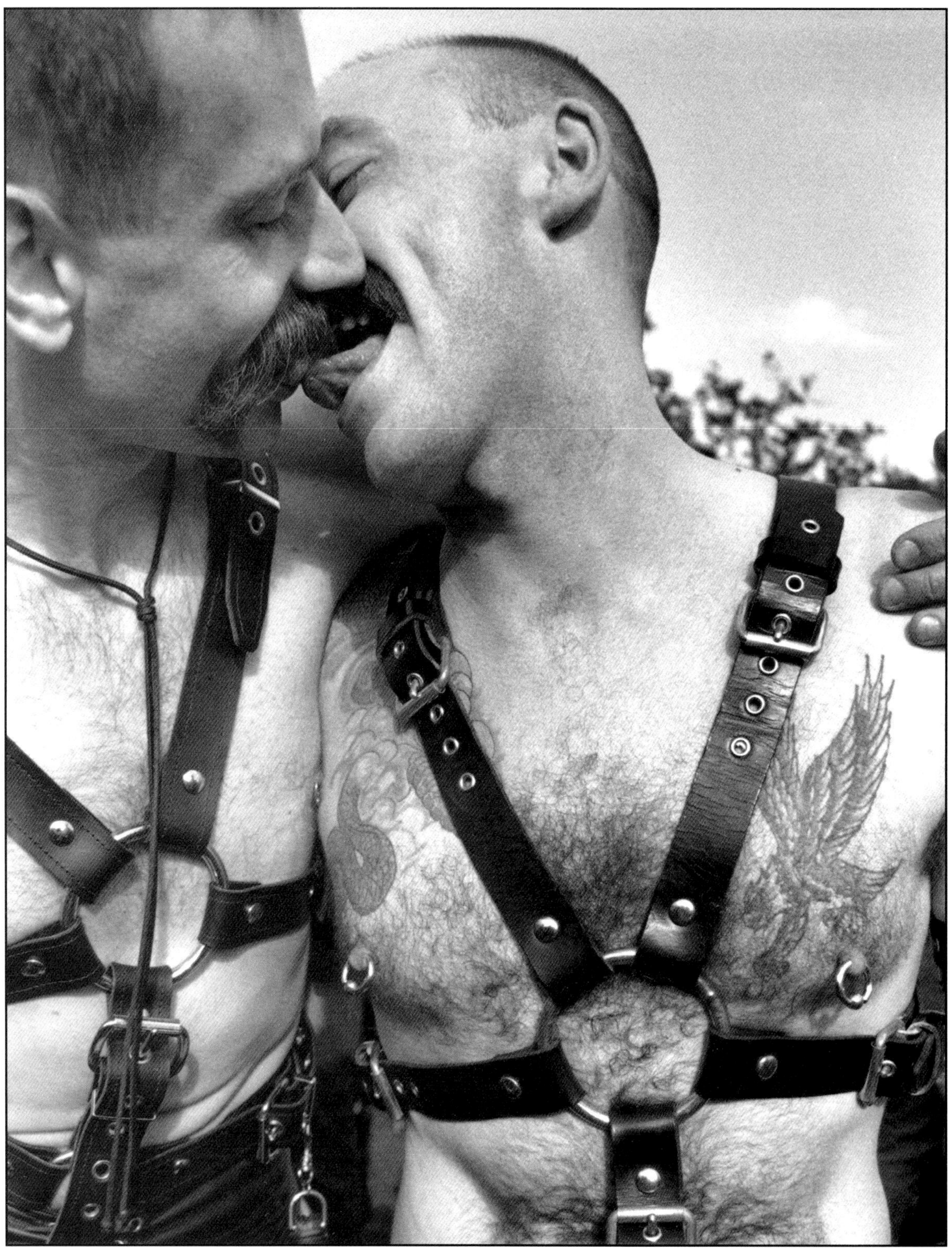

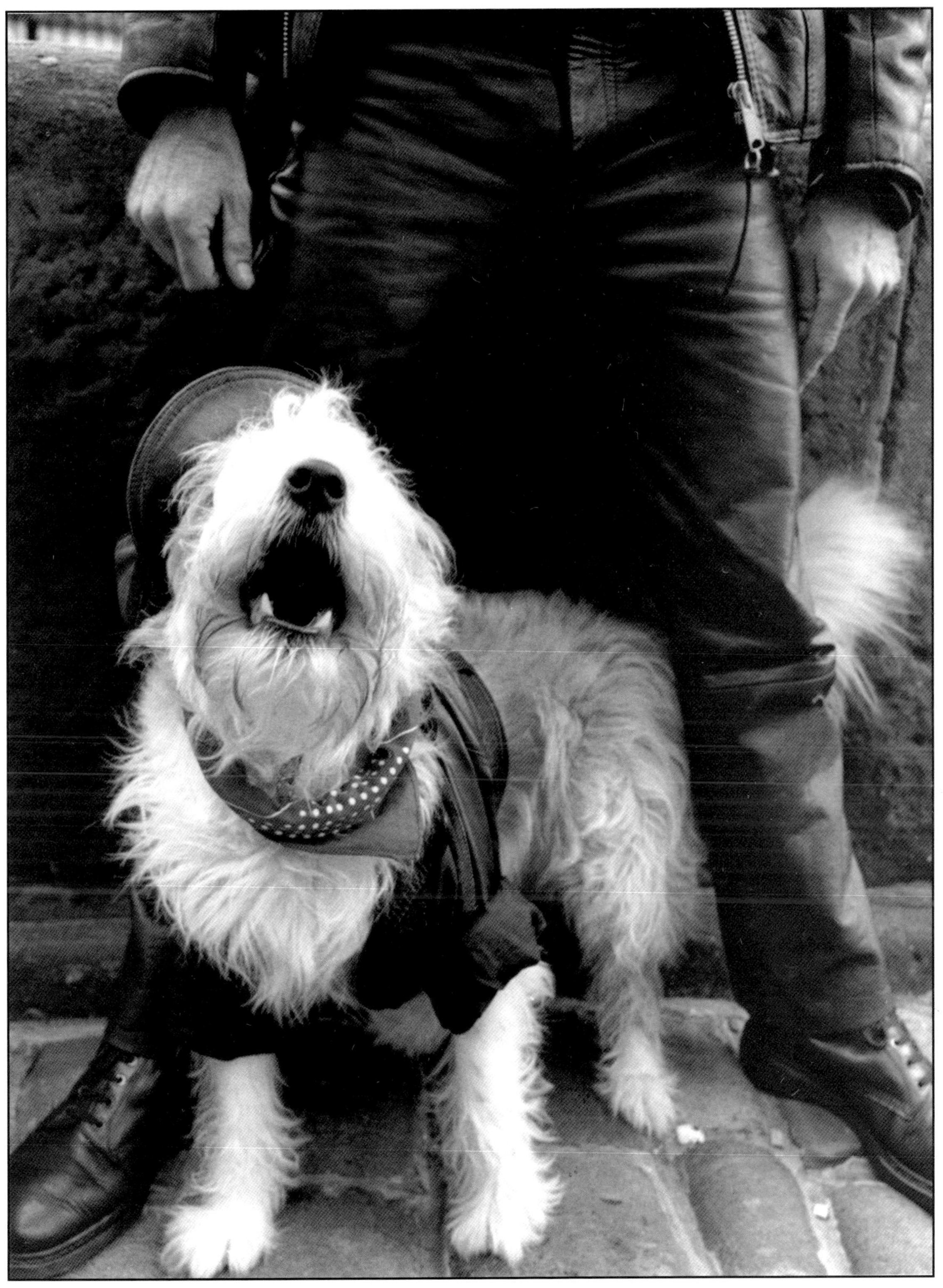

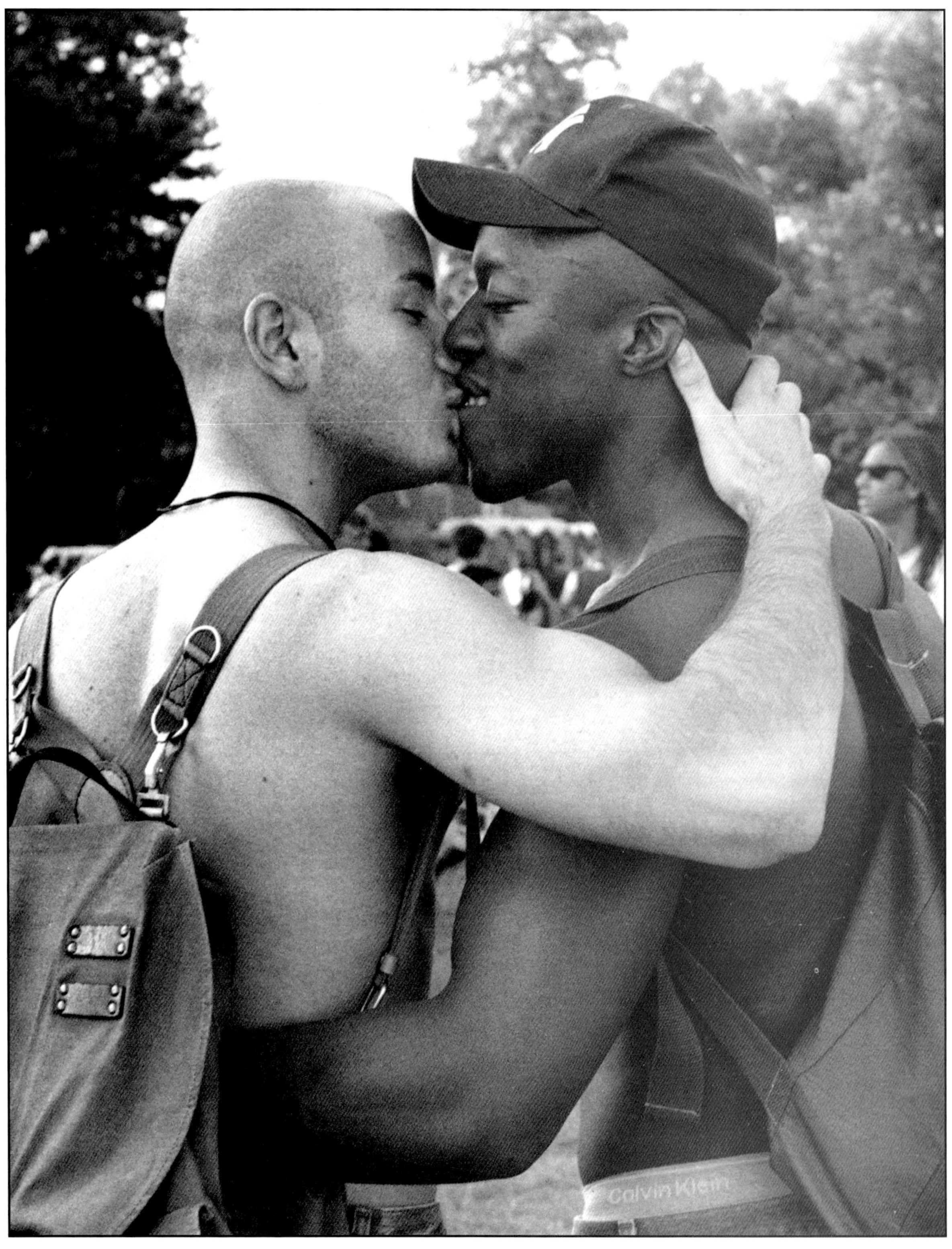

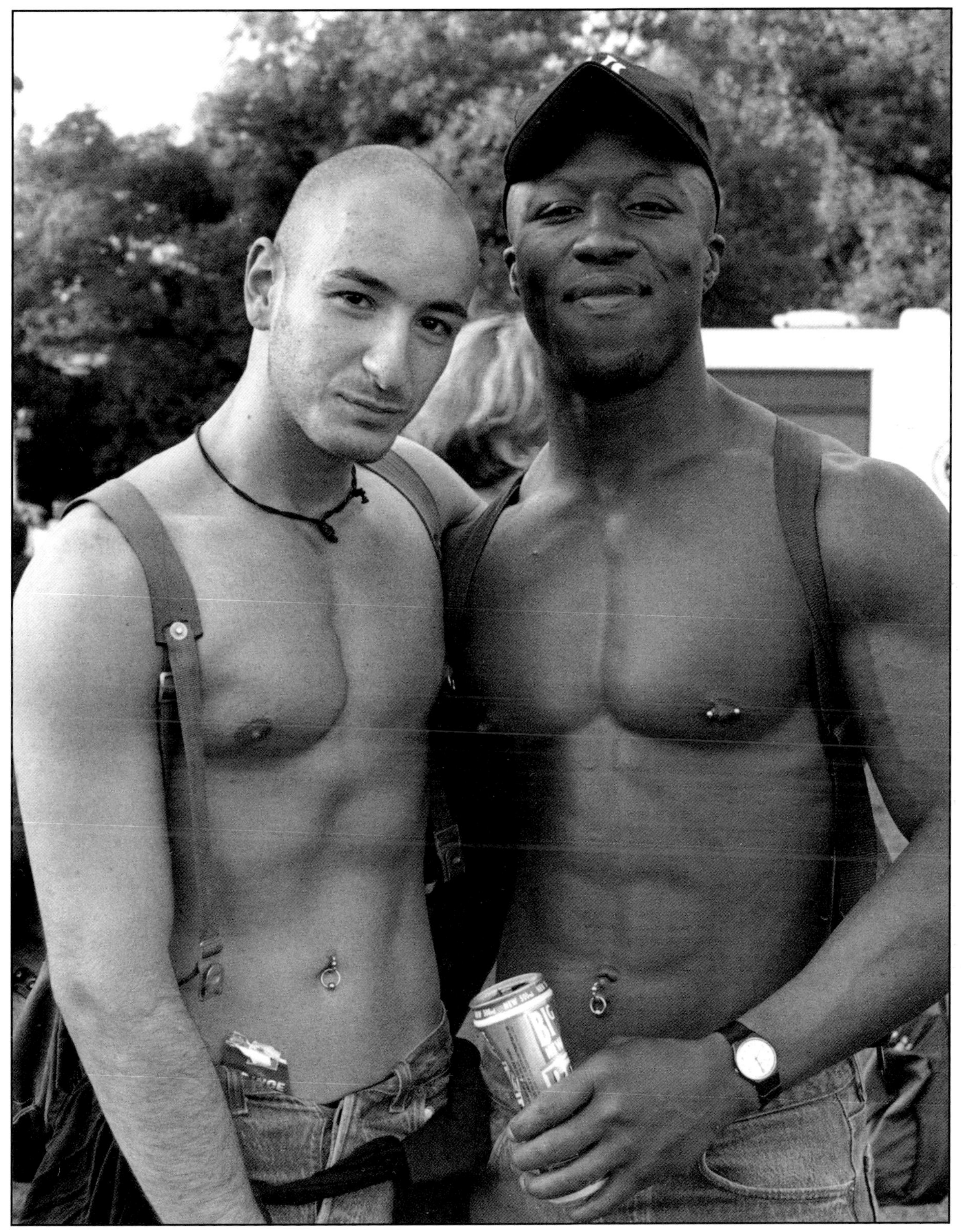

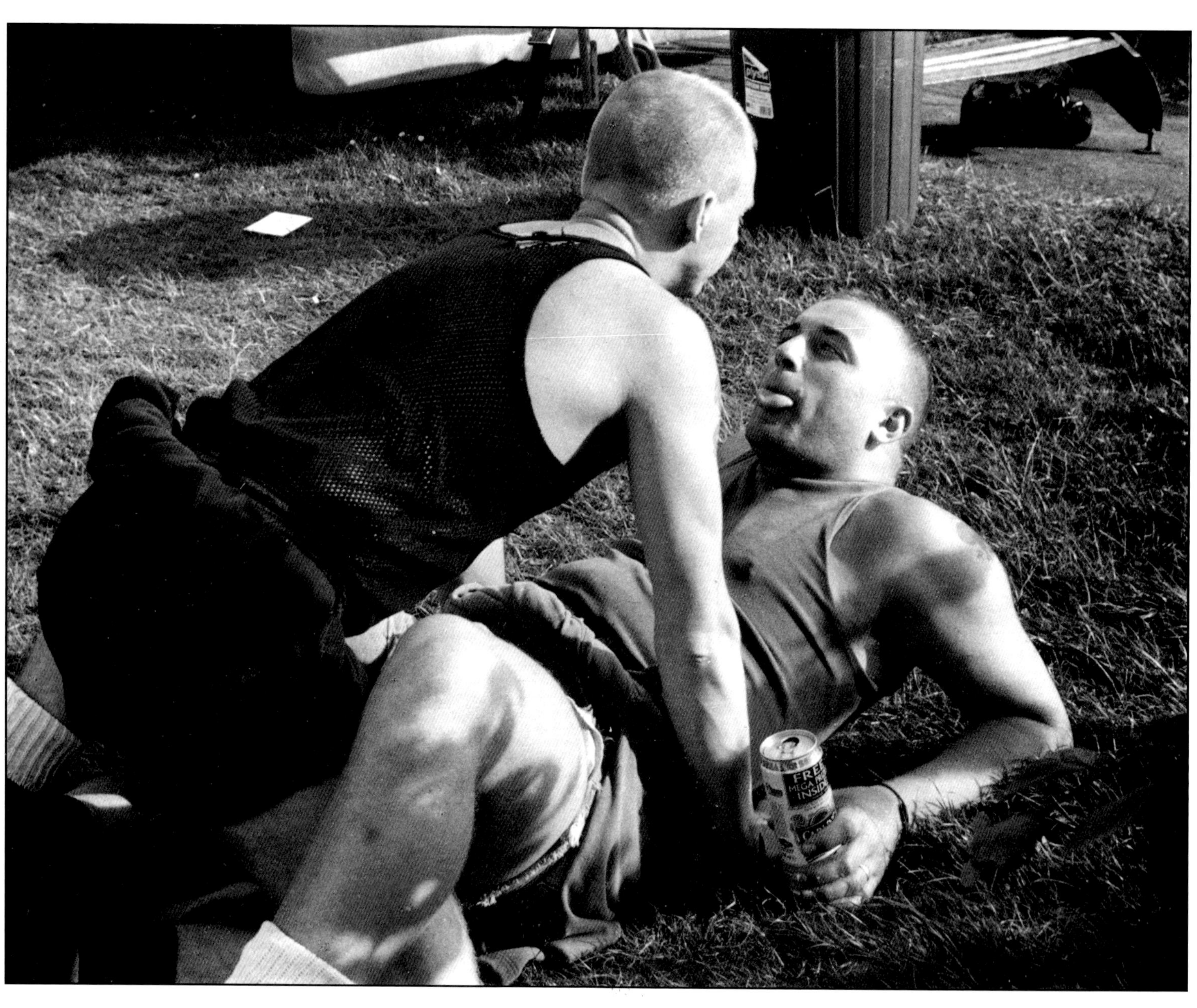

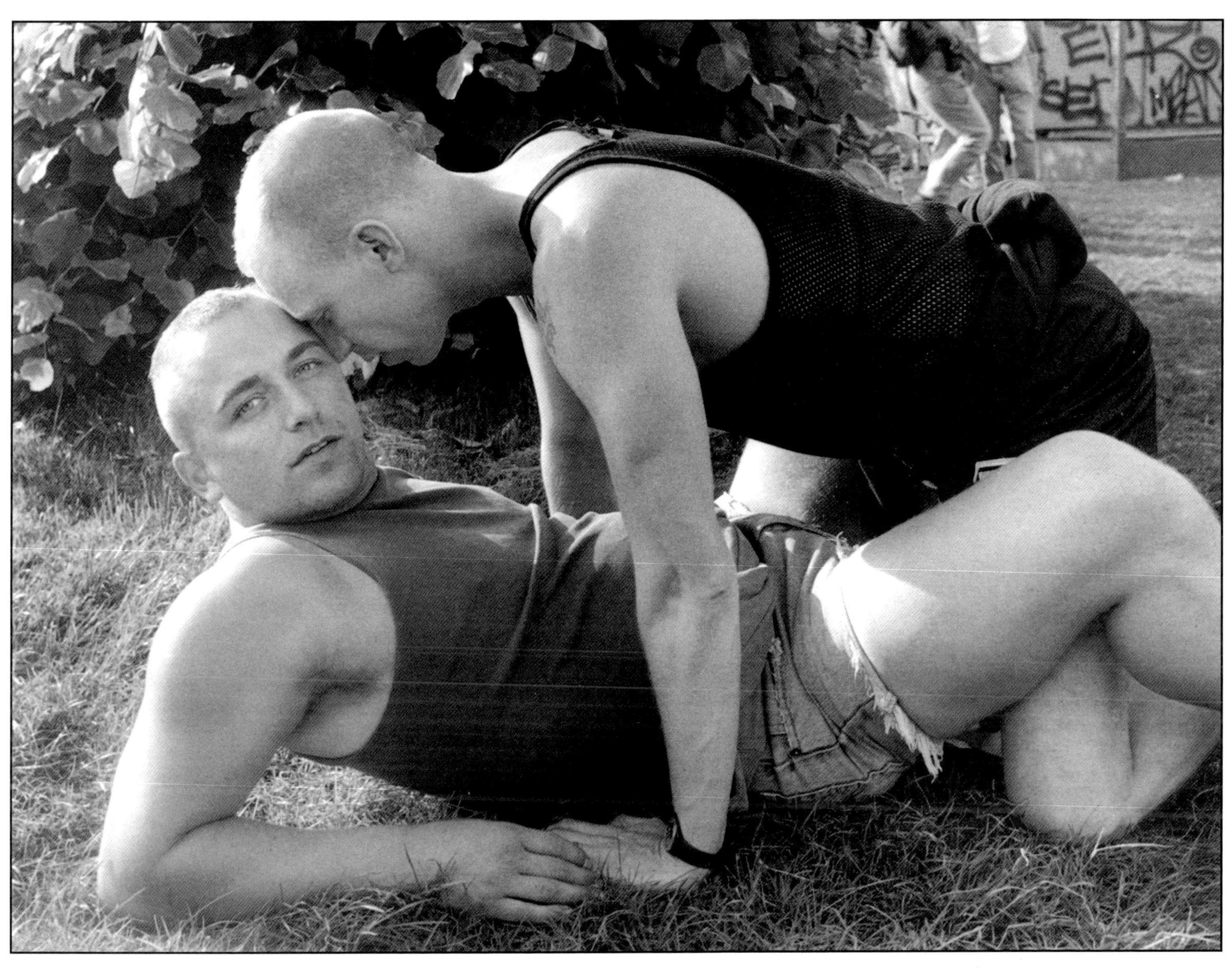

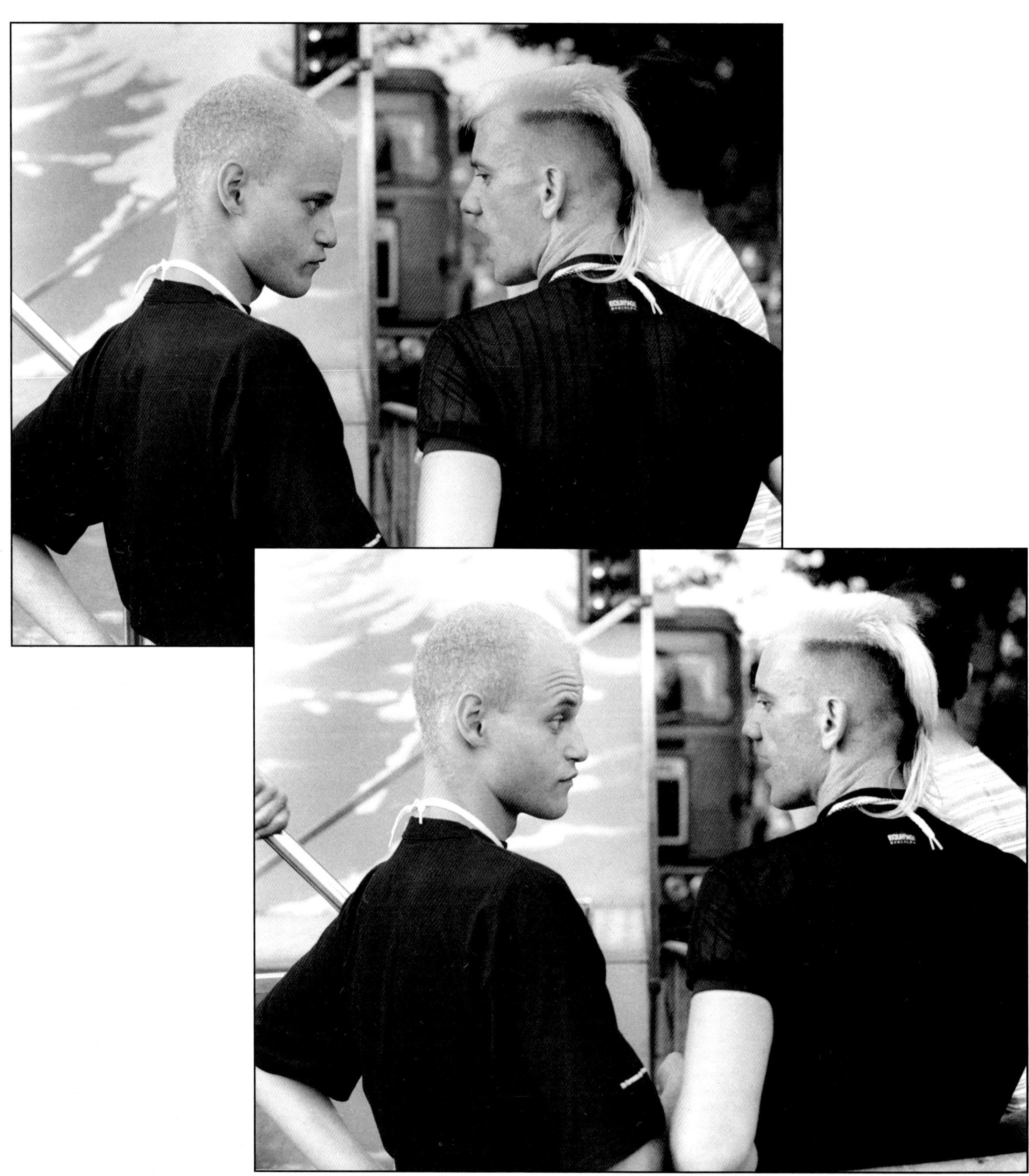

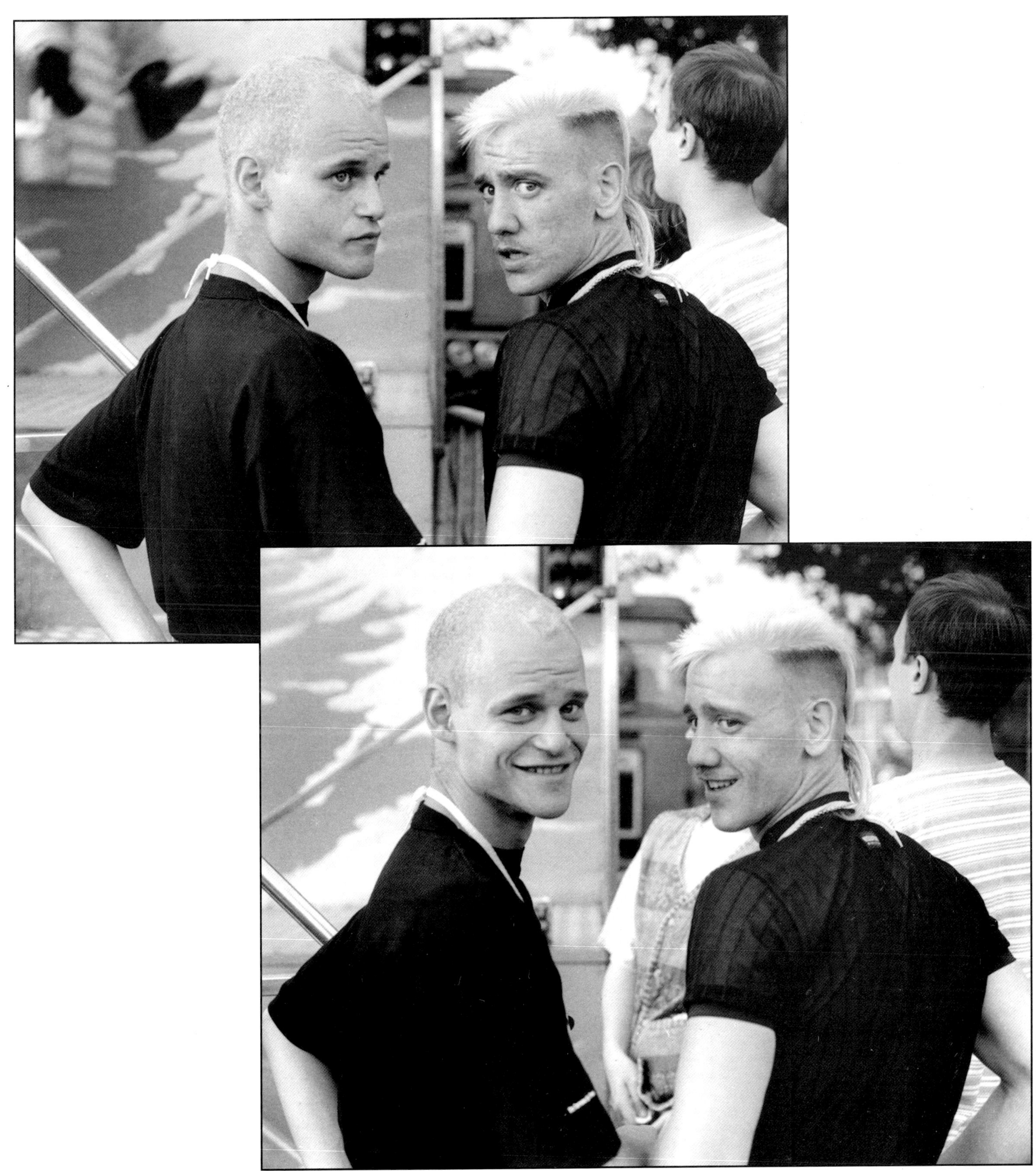

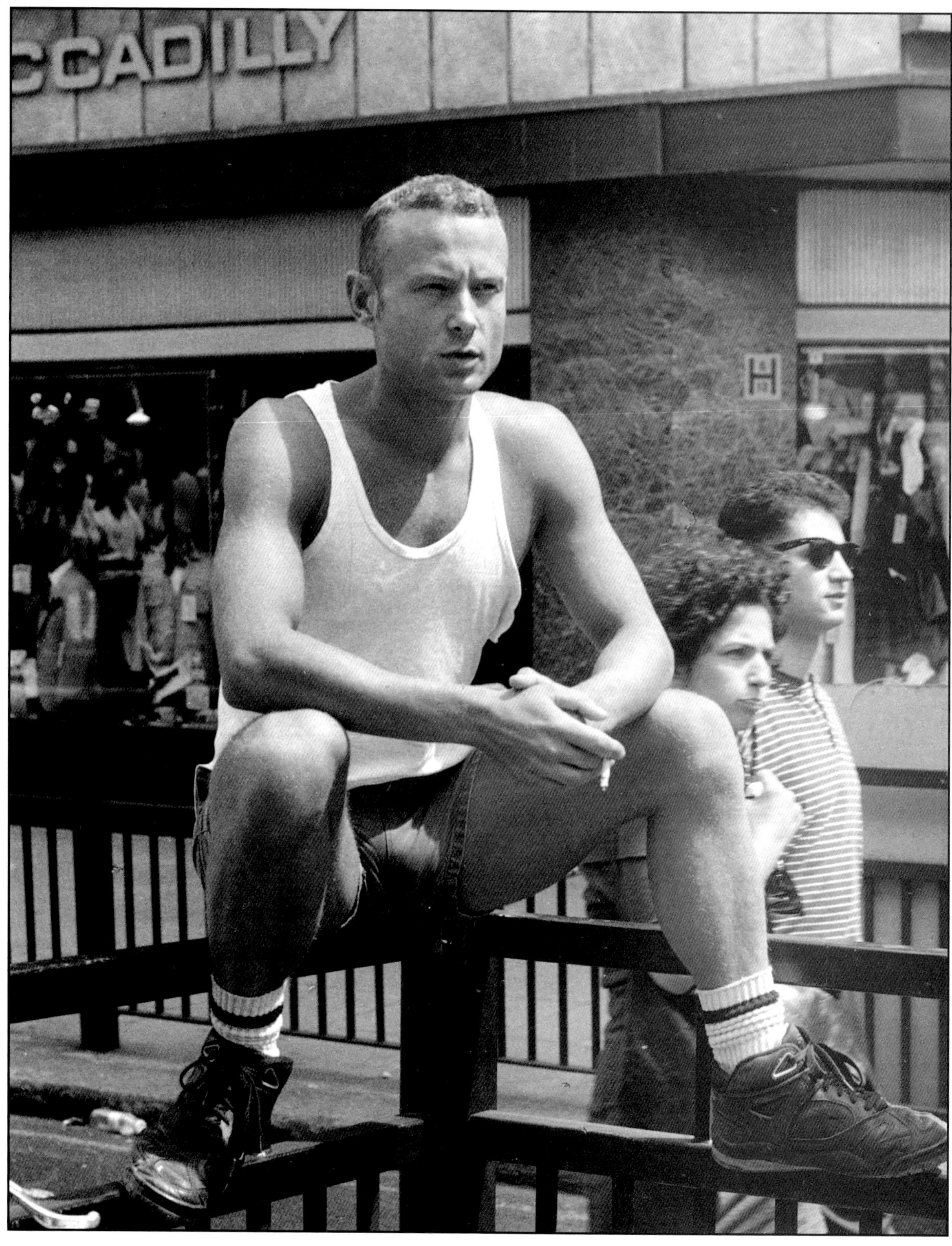
CCADILLY

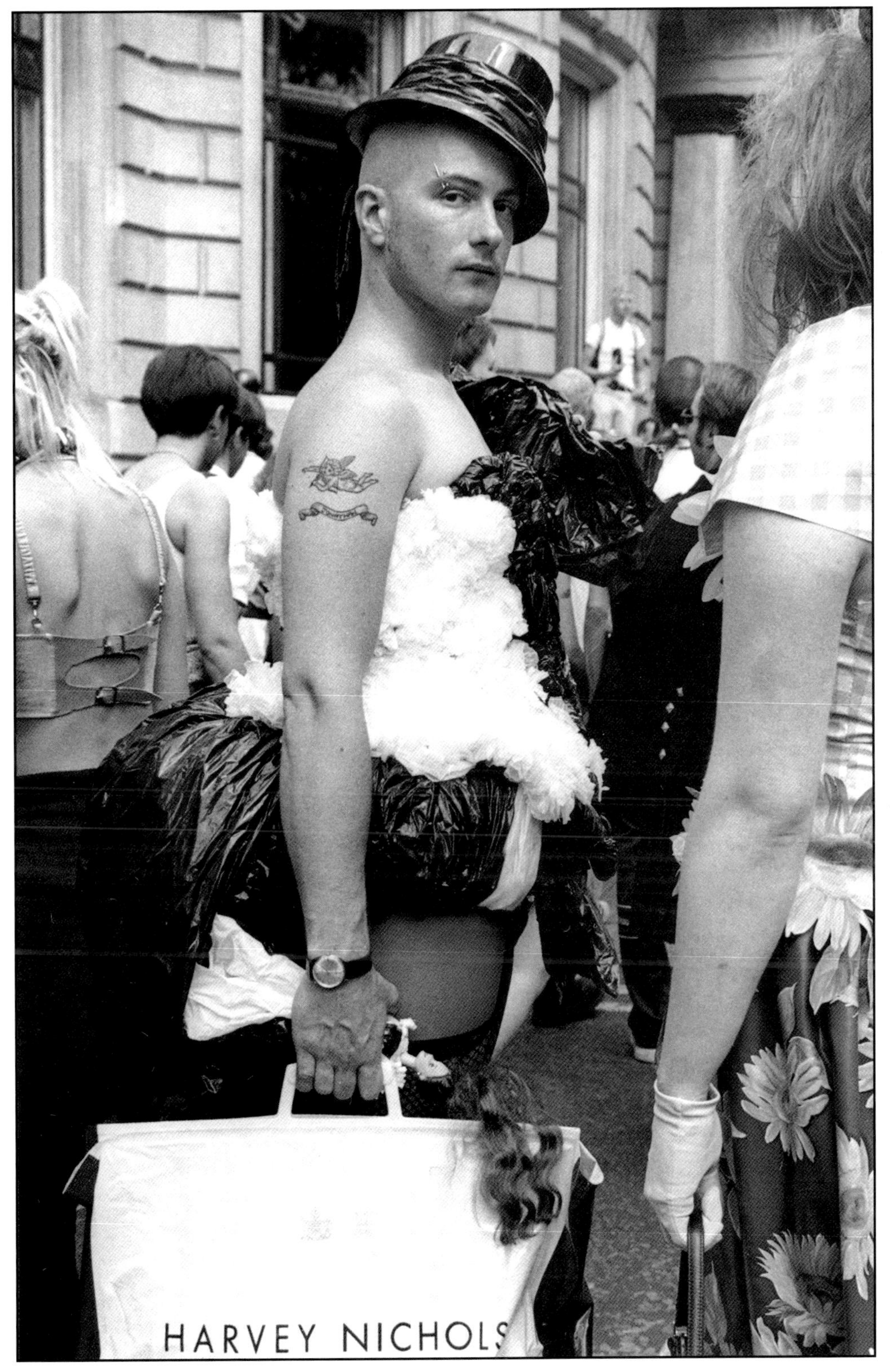

HARVEY NICHOLS

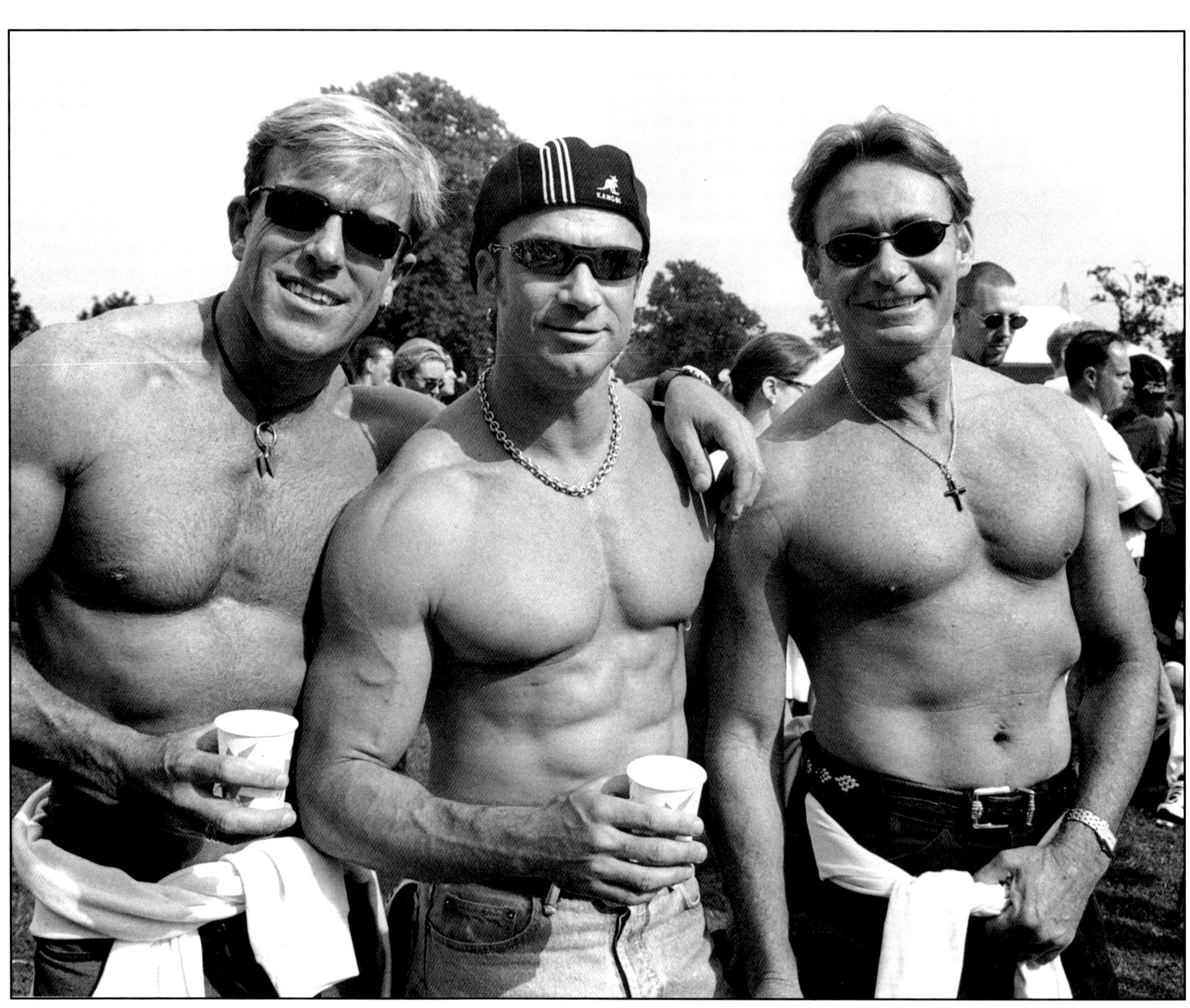

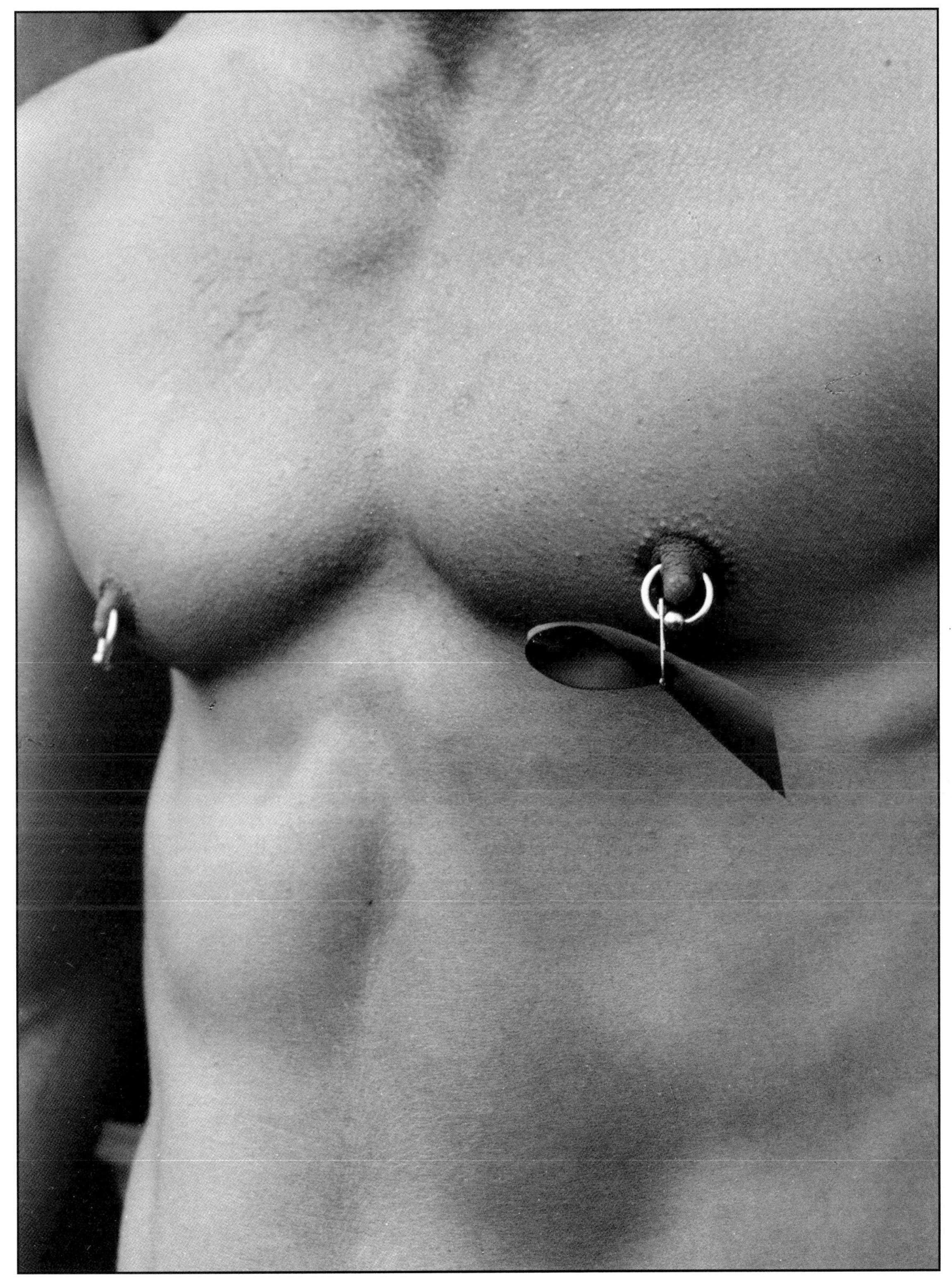

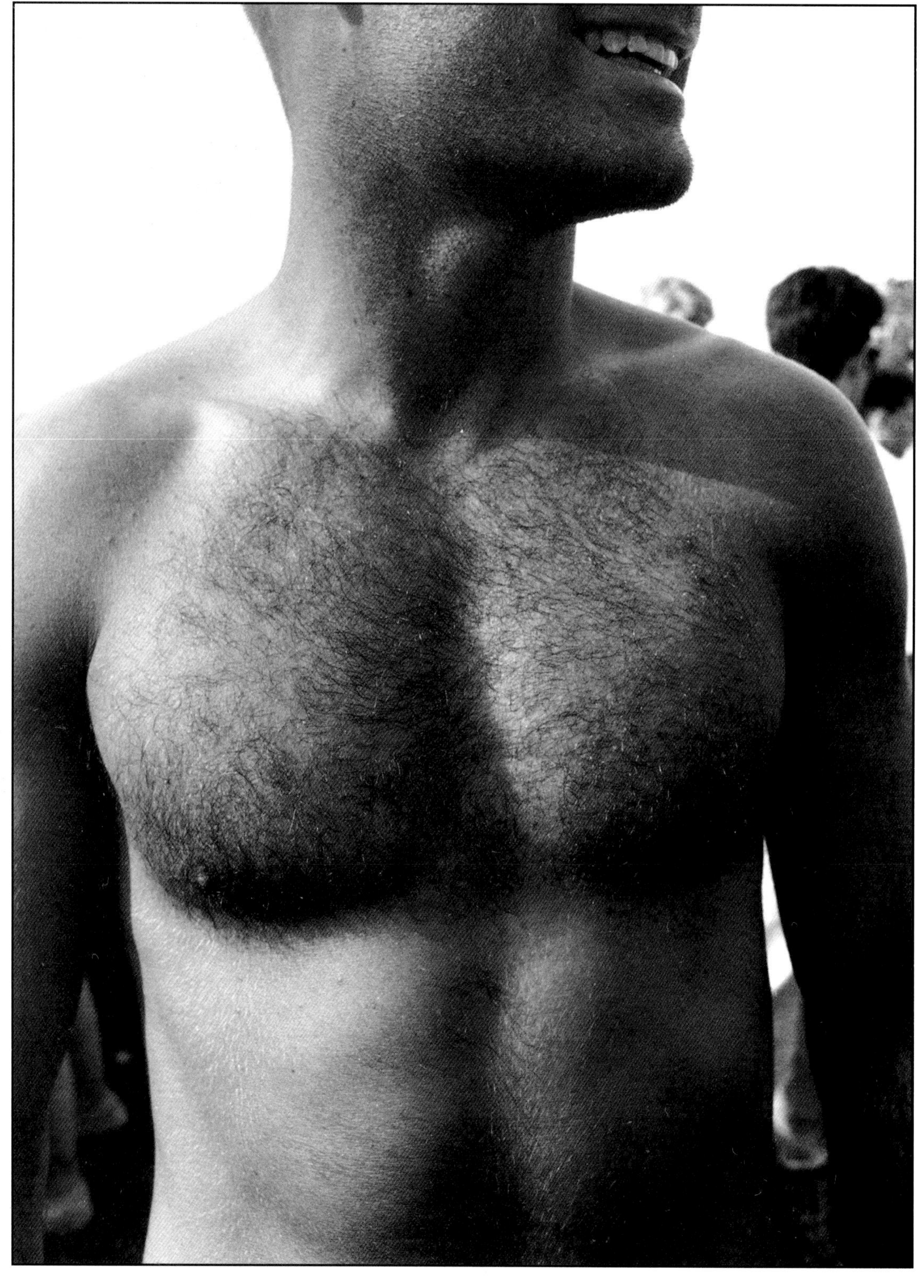

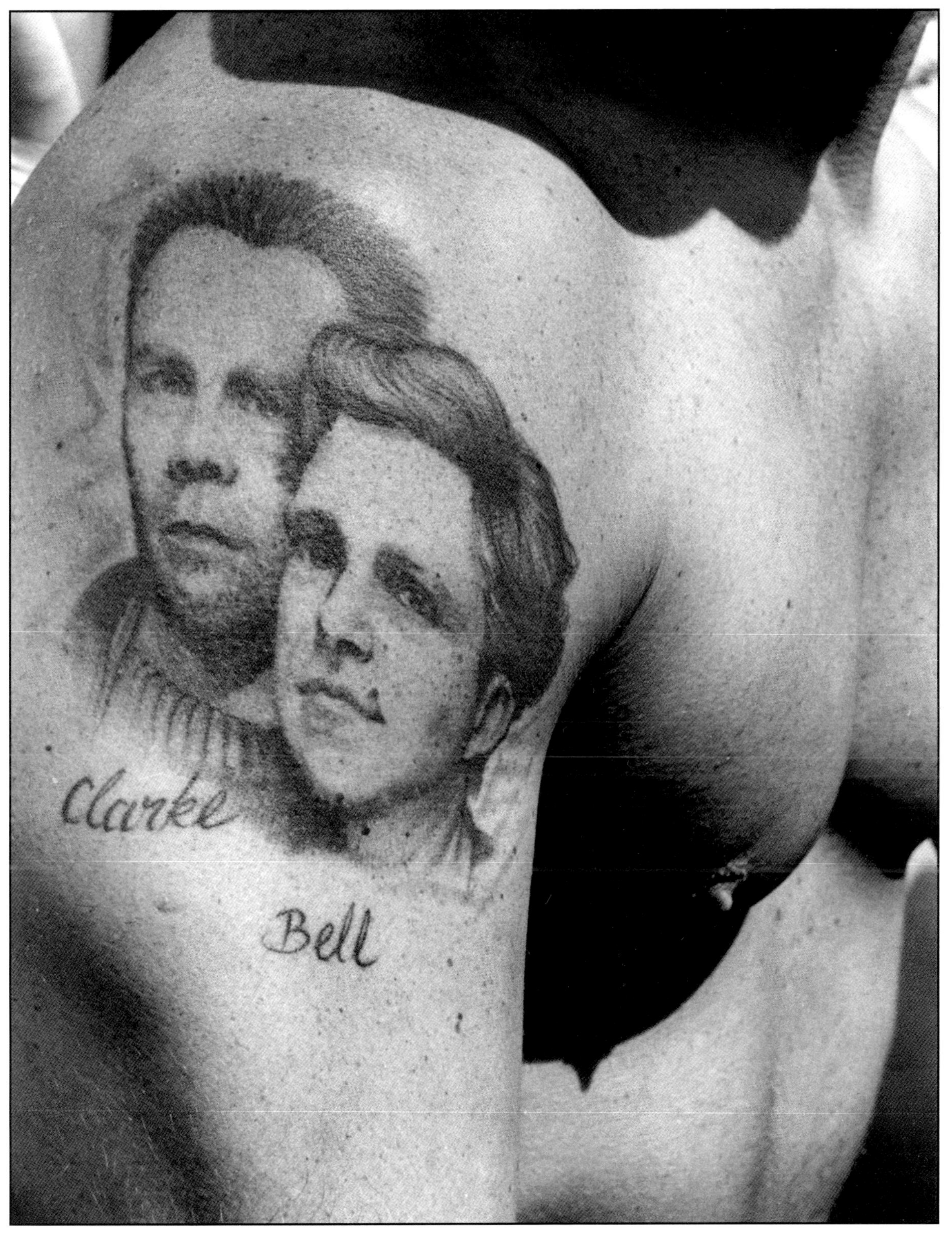

Clarke
Bell

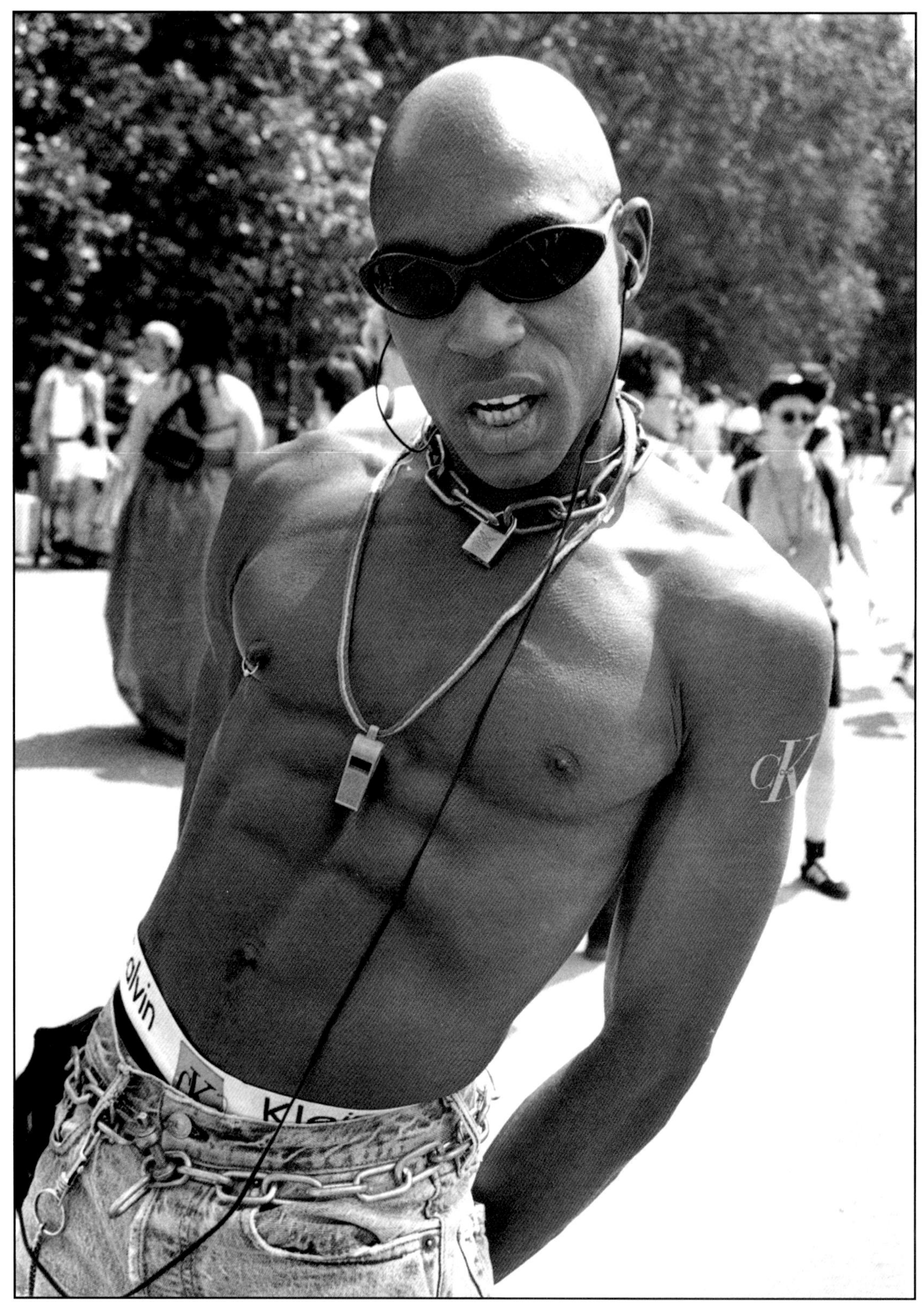

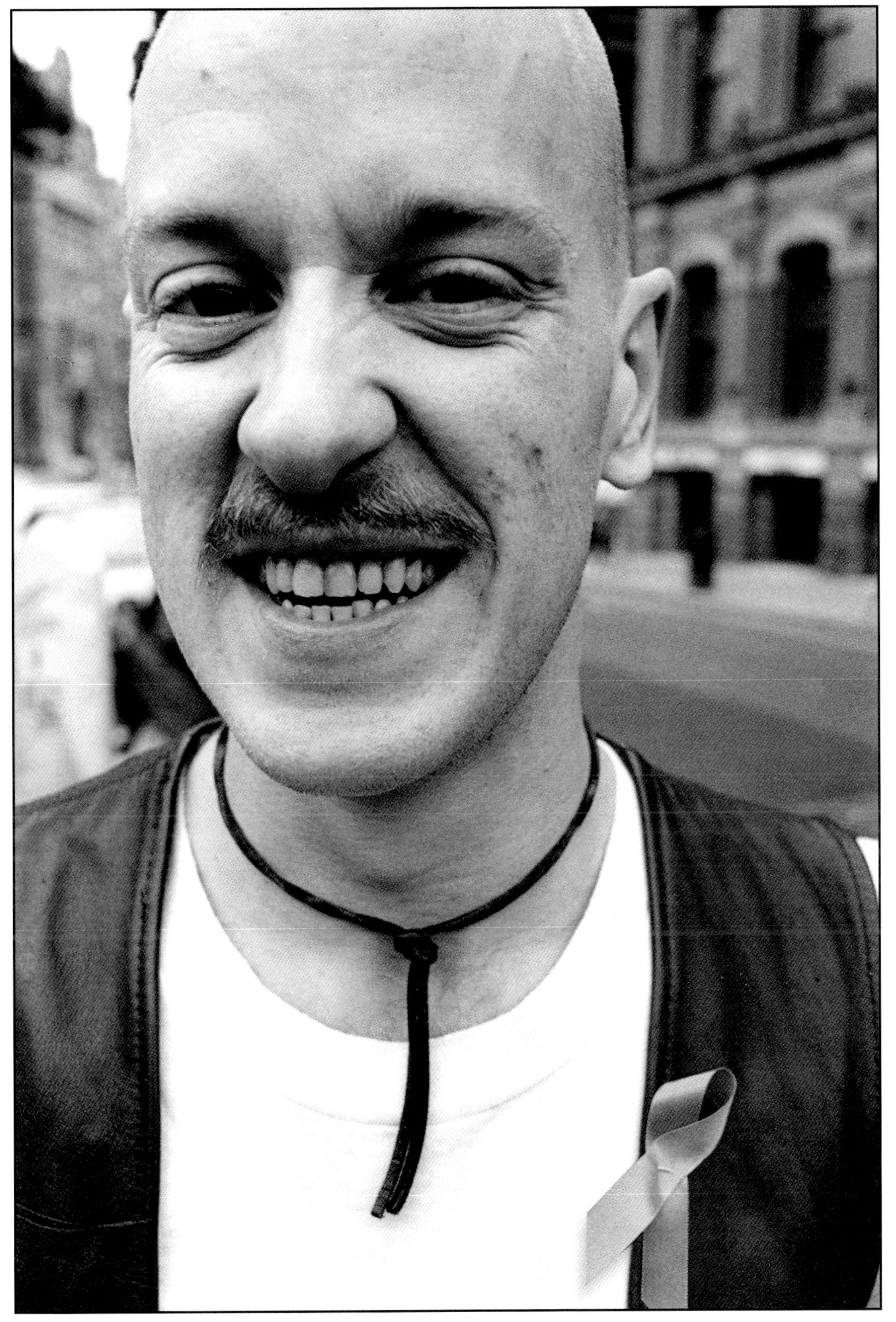

DISCOS AND PARTIES.

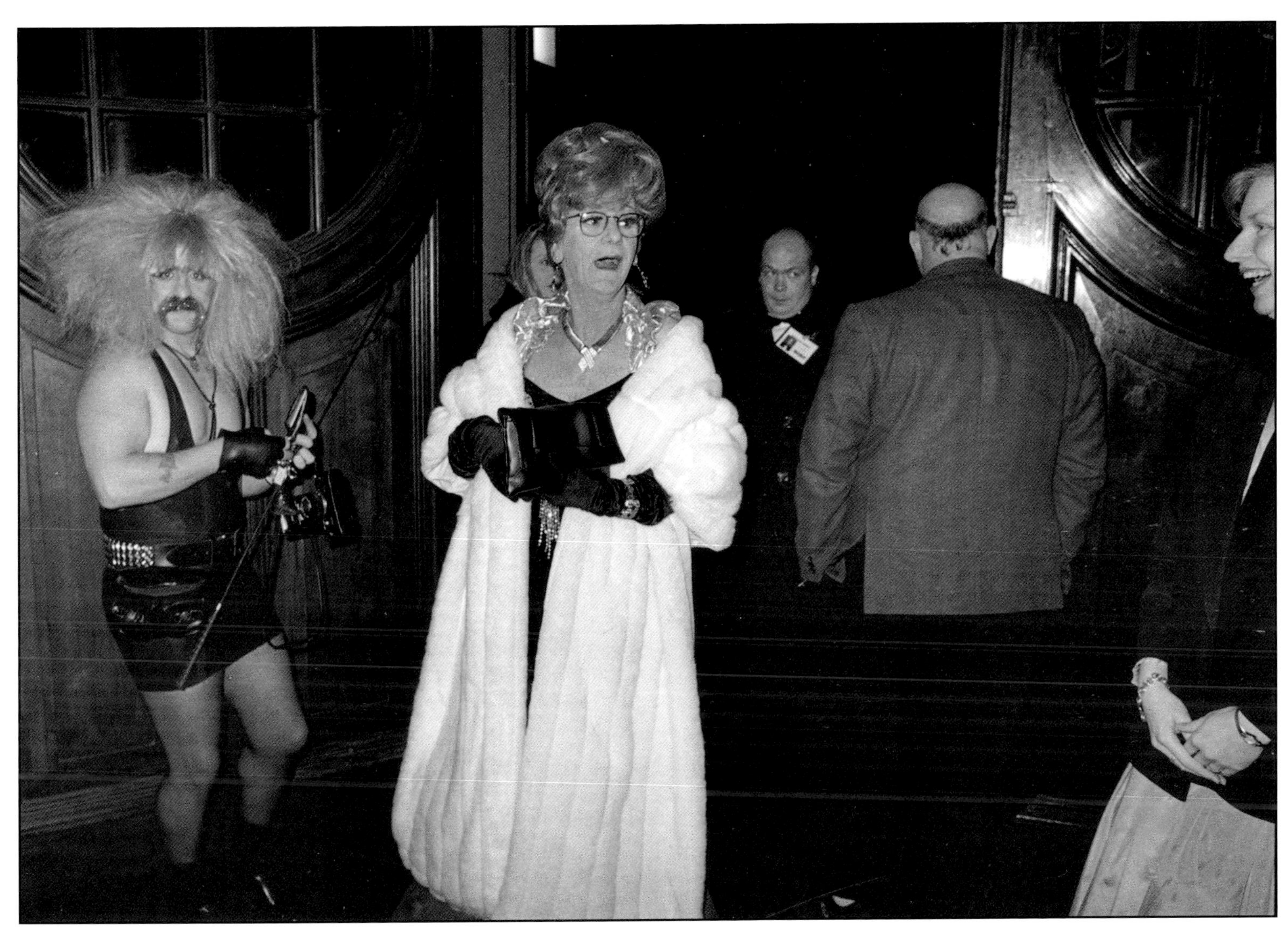

The arrival of Ray Chantelle.

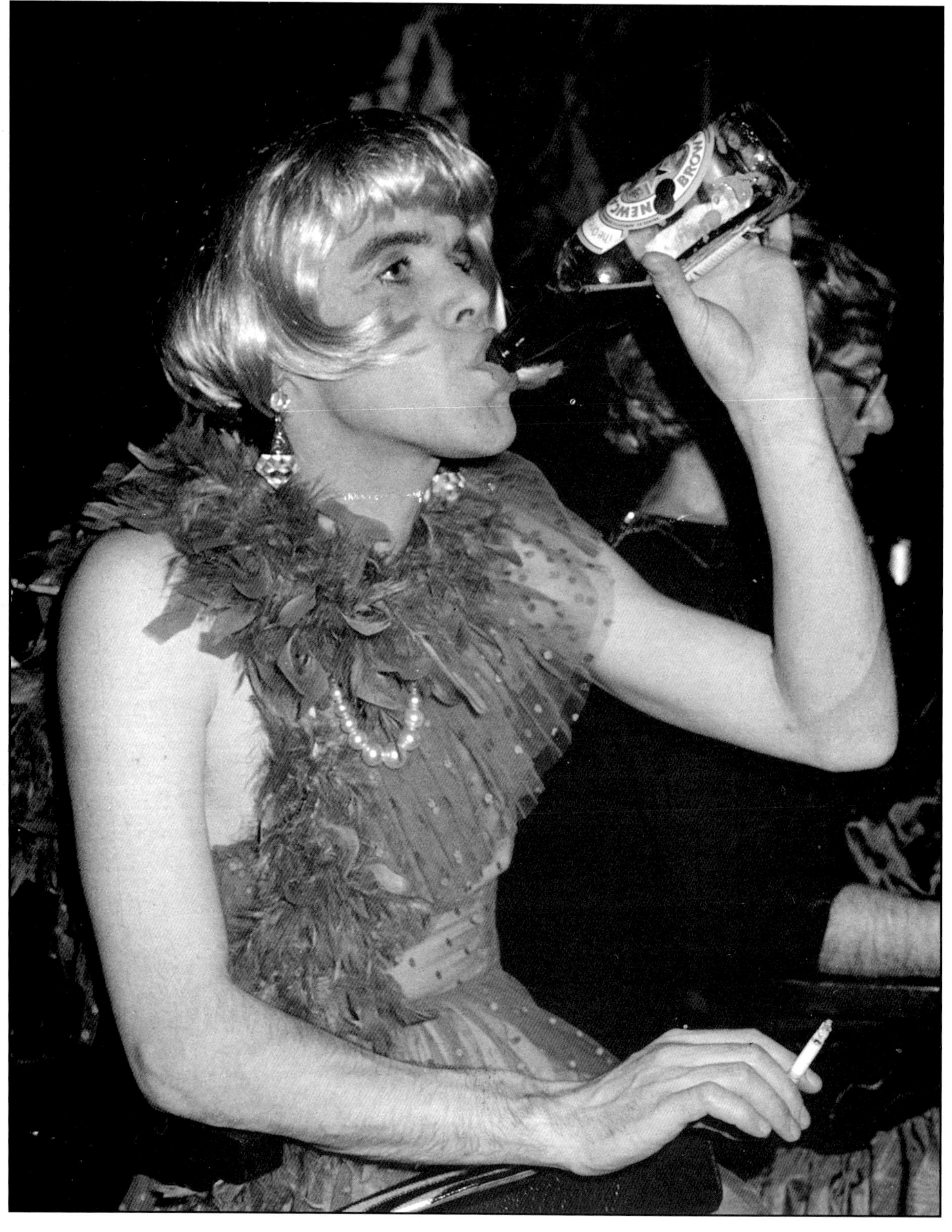

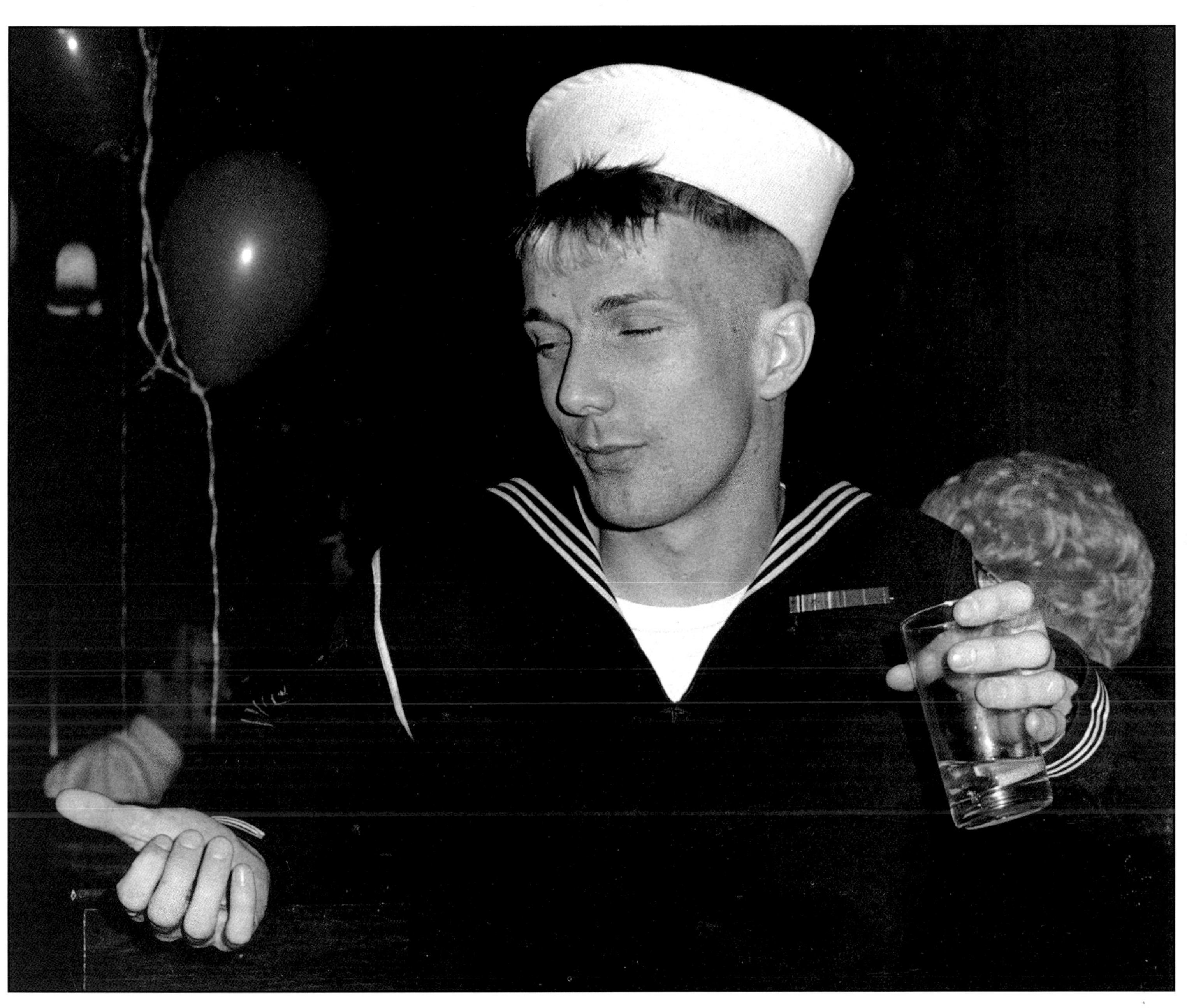

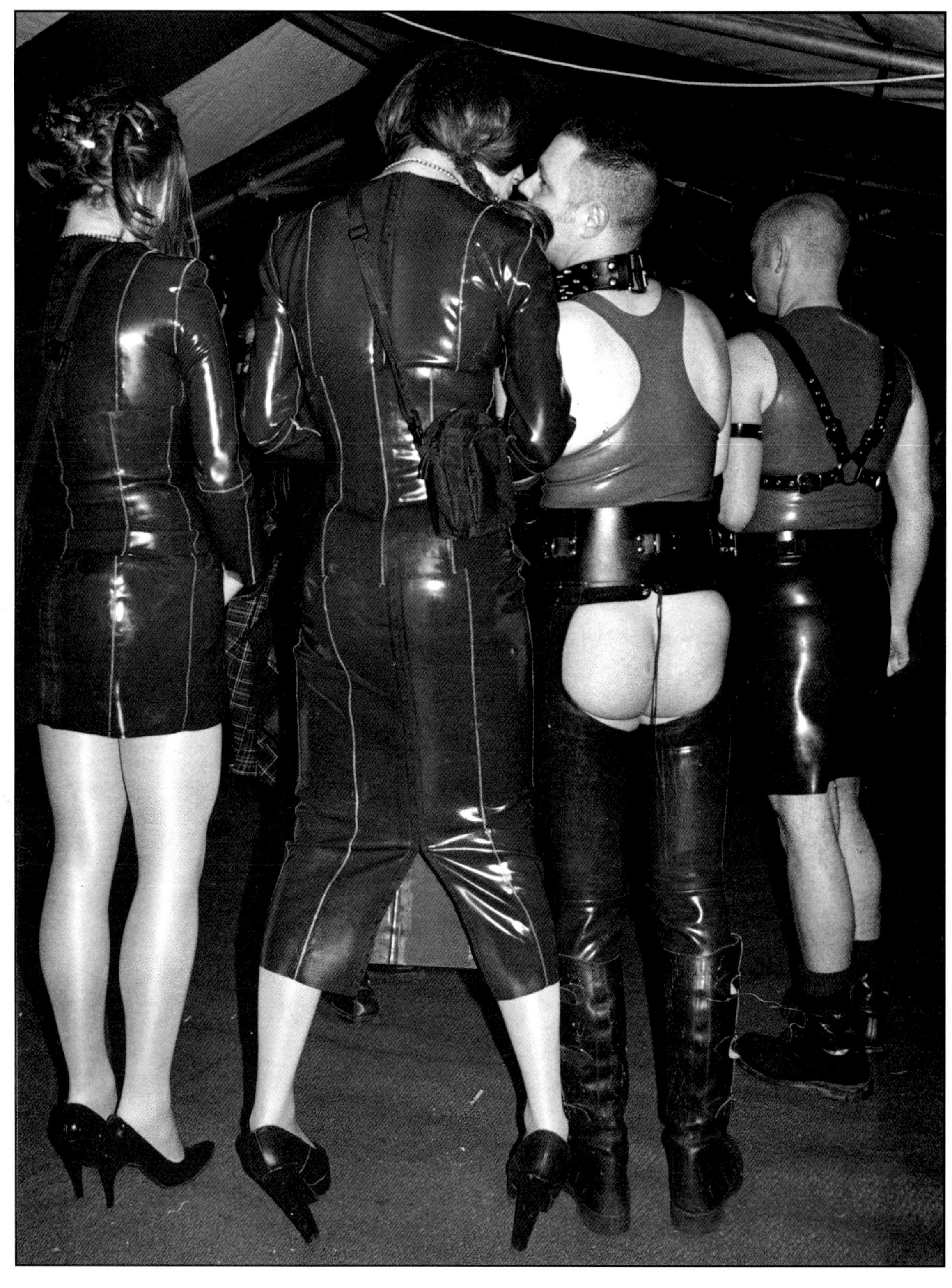

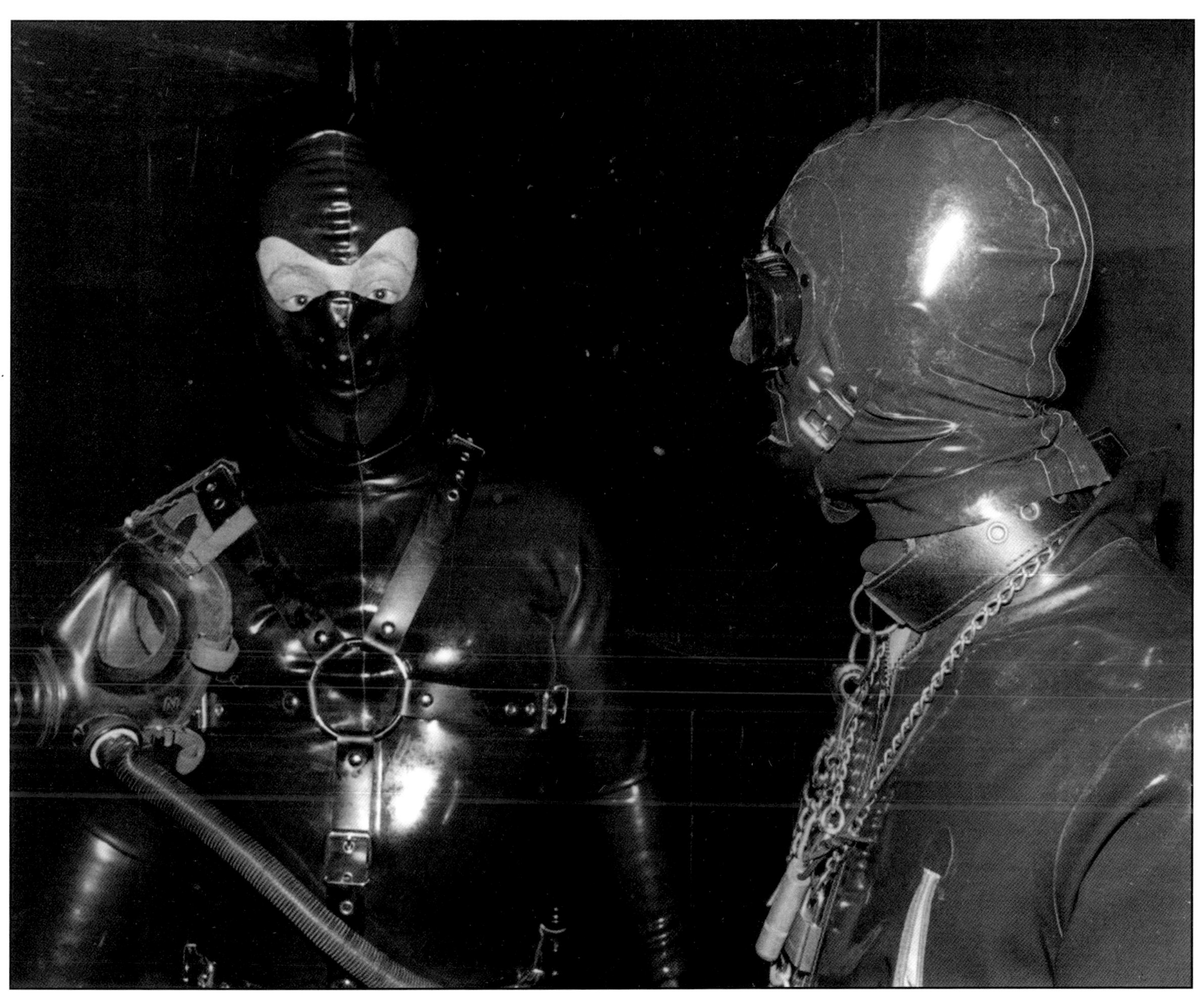

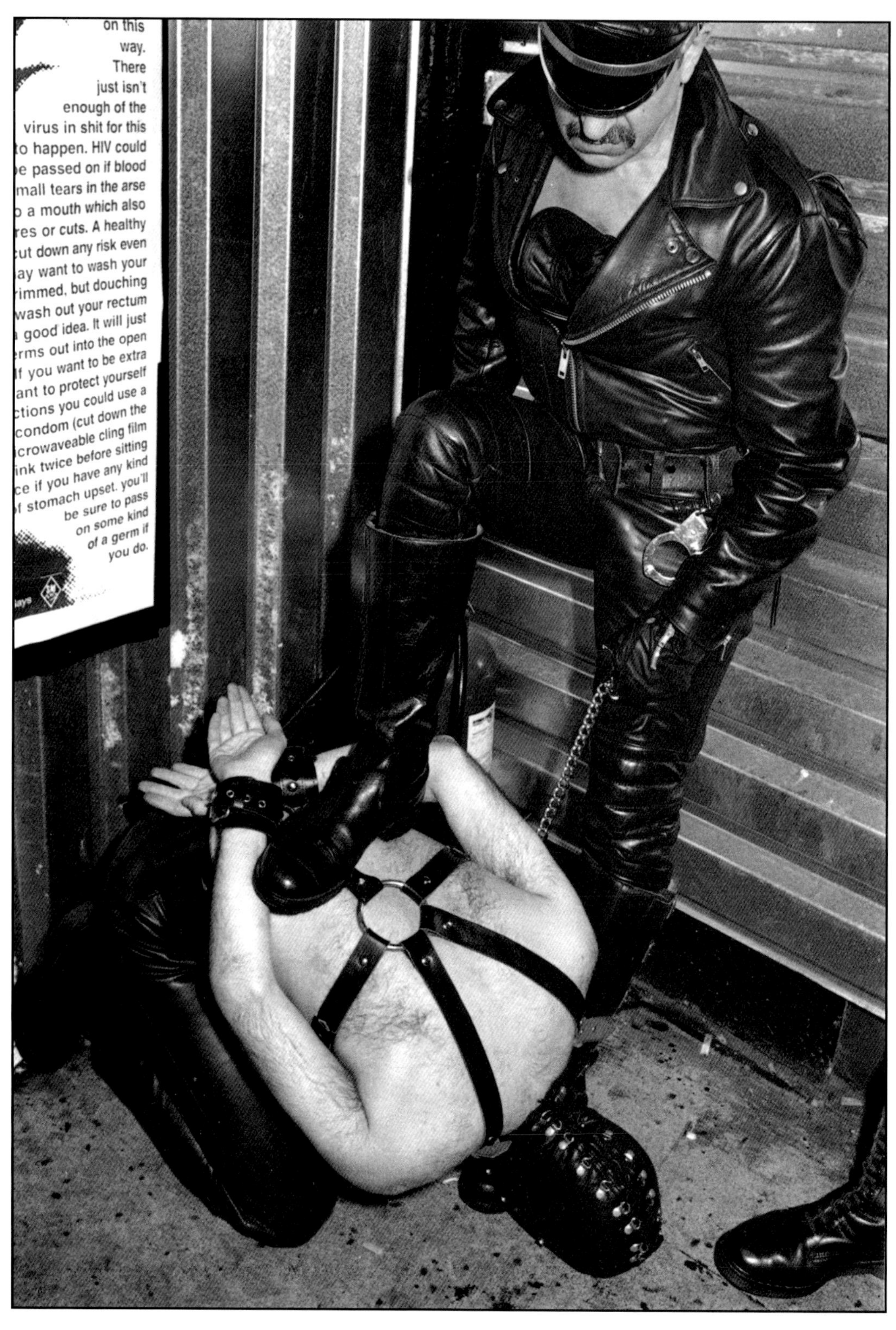

on this
way.
There
just isn't
enough of the
virus in shit for this
to happen. HIV could
be passed on if blood
small tears in the arse
to a mouth which also
sores or cuts. A healthy
cut down any risk even
may want to wash your
rimmed, but douching
wash out your rectum
good idea. It will just
germs out into the open
If you want to be extra
ant to protect yourself
actions you could use a
condom (cut down the
microwaveable cling film
drink twice before sitting
ce if you have any kind
of stomach upset. you'll
be sure to pass
on some kind
of a germ if
you do.

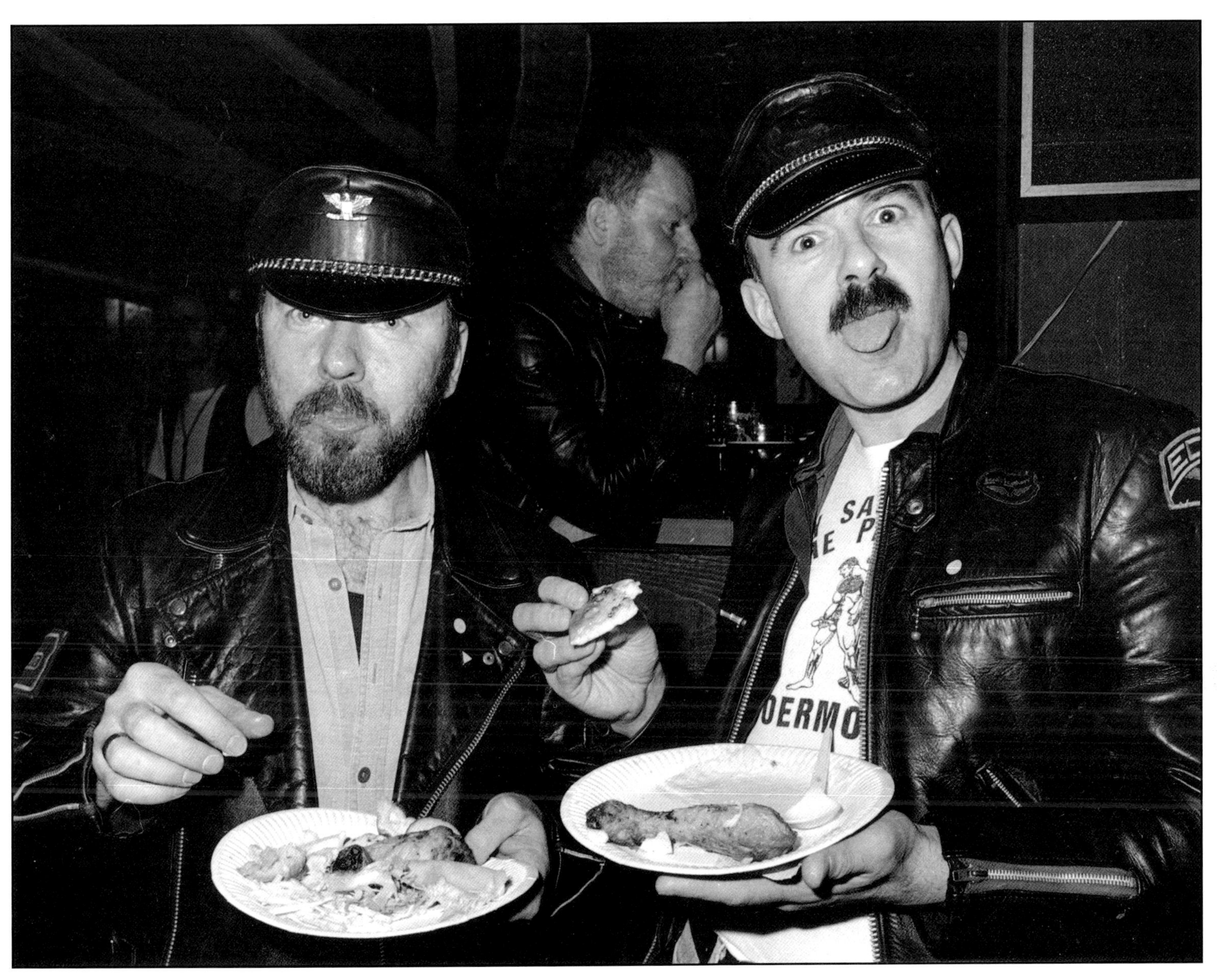

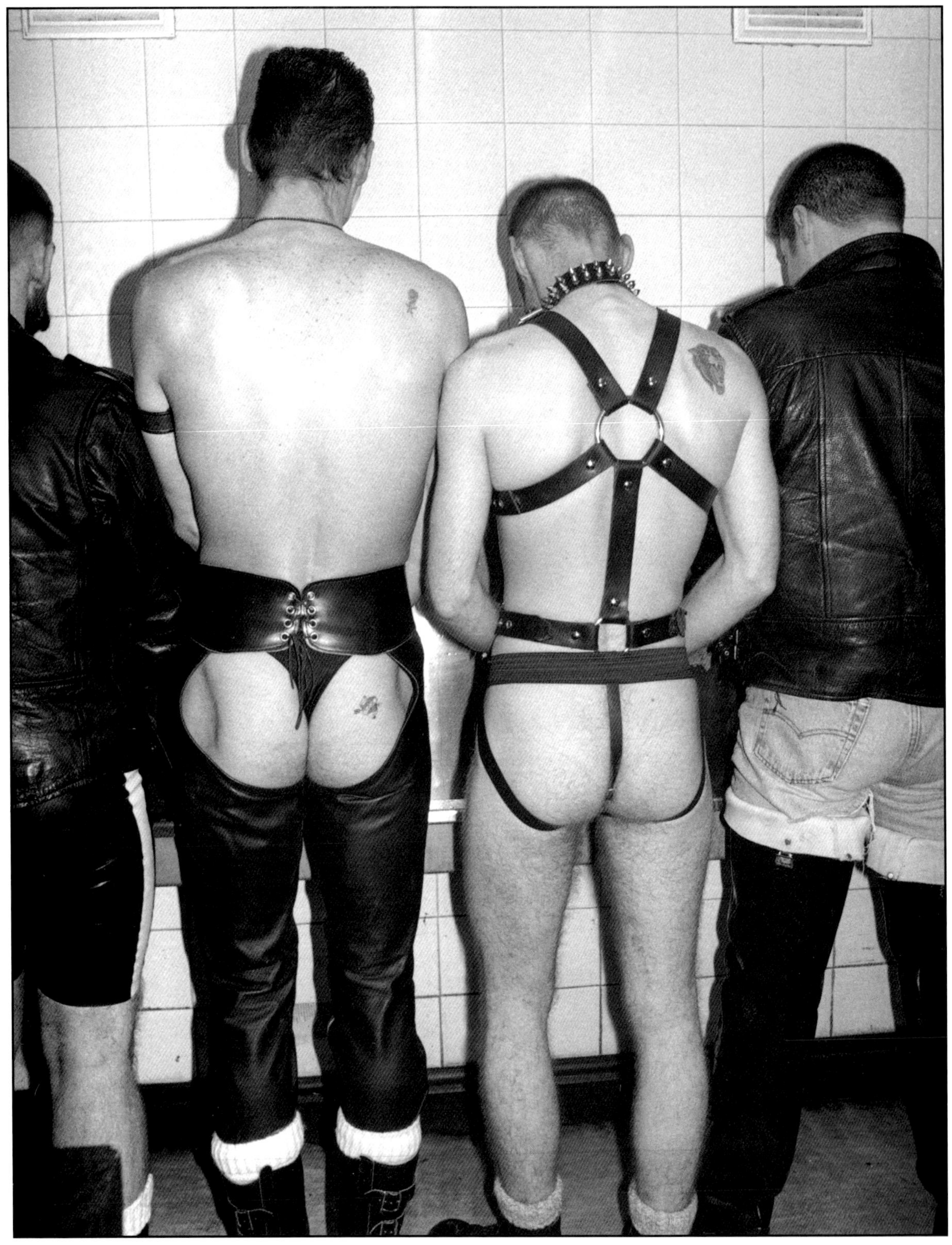

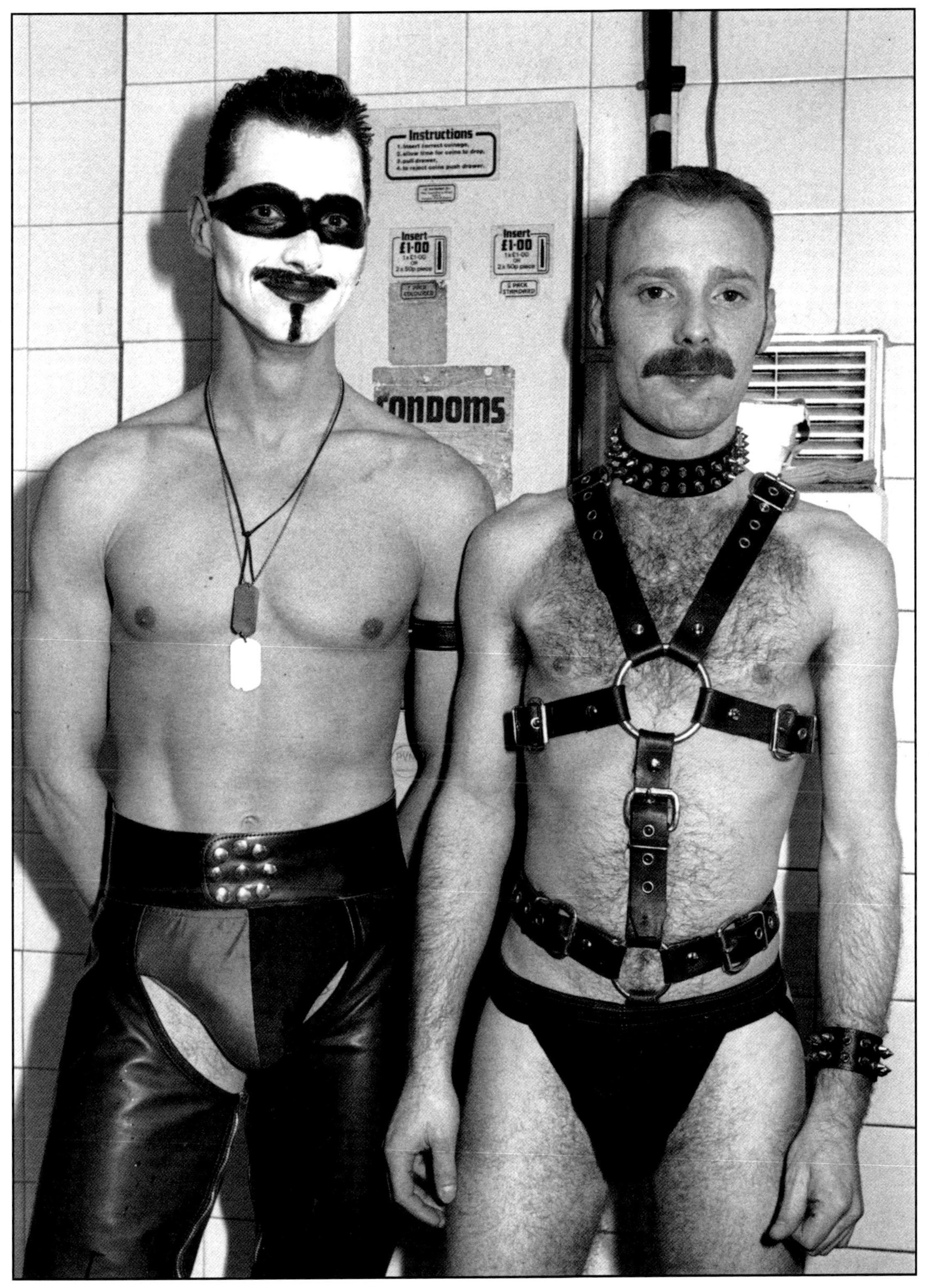
Instructions
1. Insert correct coinage.
2. Allow time for coins to drop.
3. Pull drawer.
4. To reject coins push drawer.
Insert £1·00
1 x £1·00
or
2 x 50p piece
Insert £1·00
1 x £1·00
or
2 x 50p piece
CONDOMS

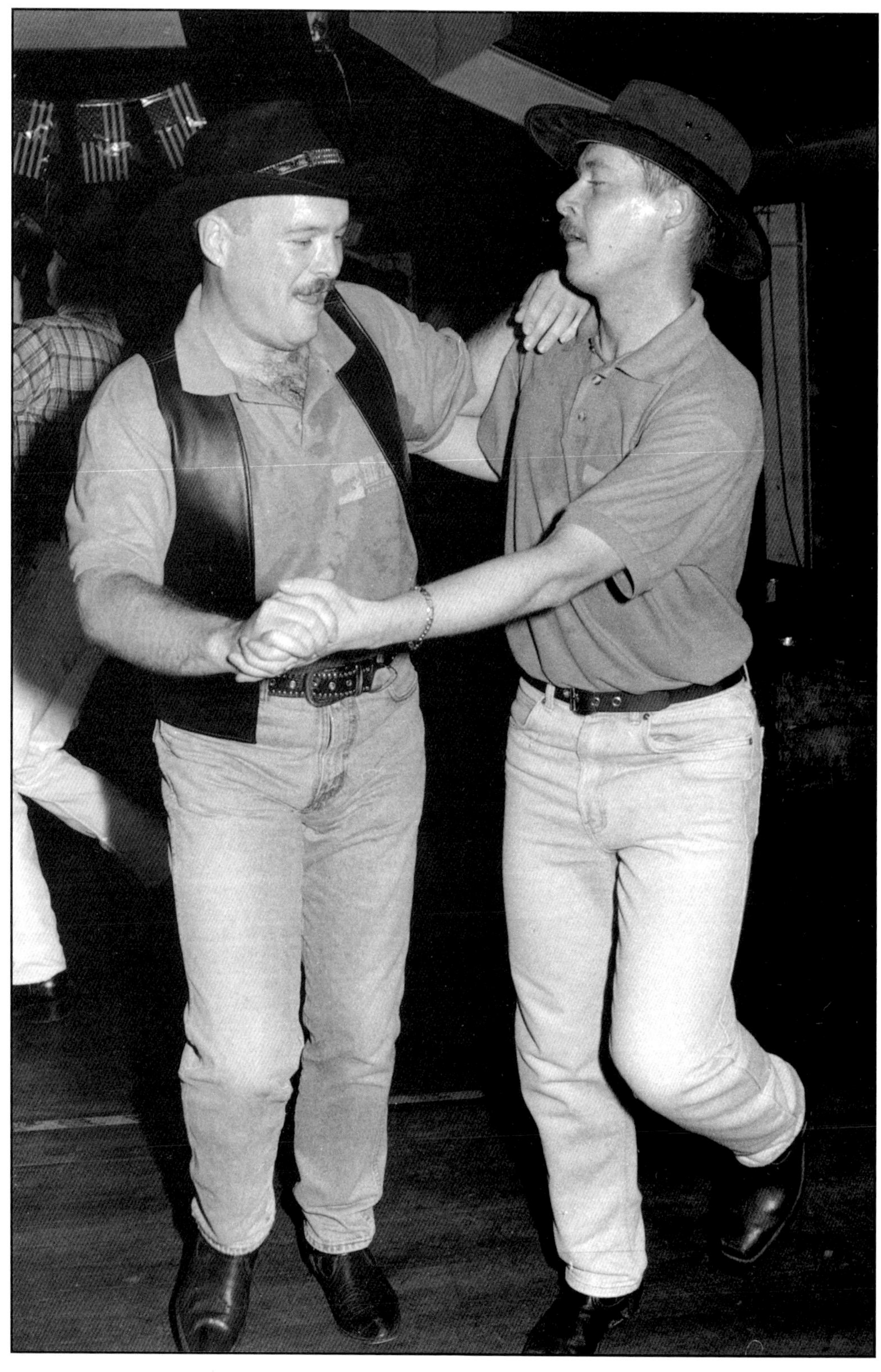

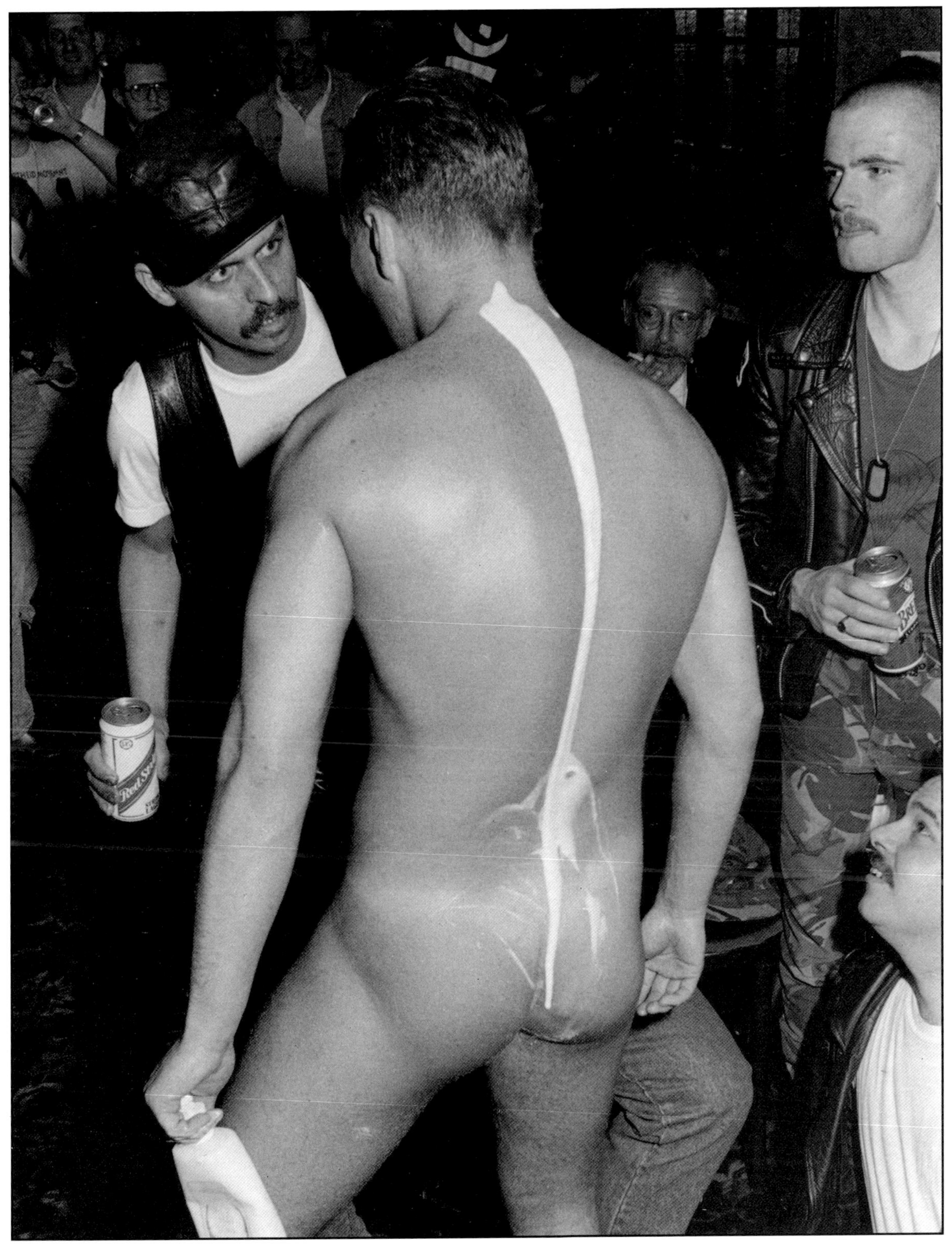

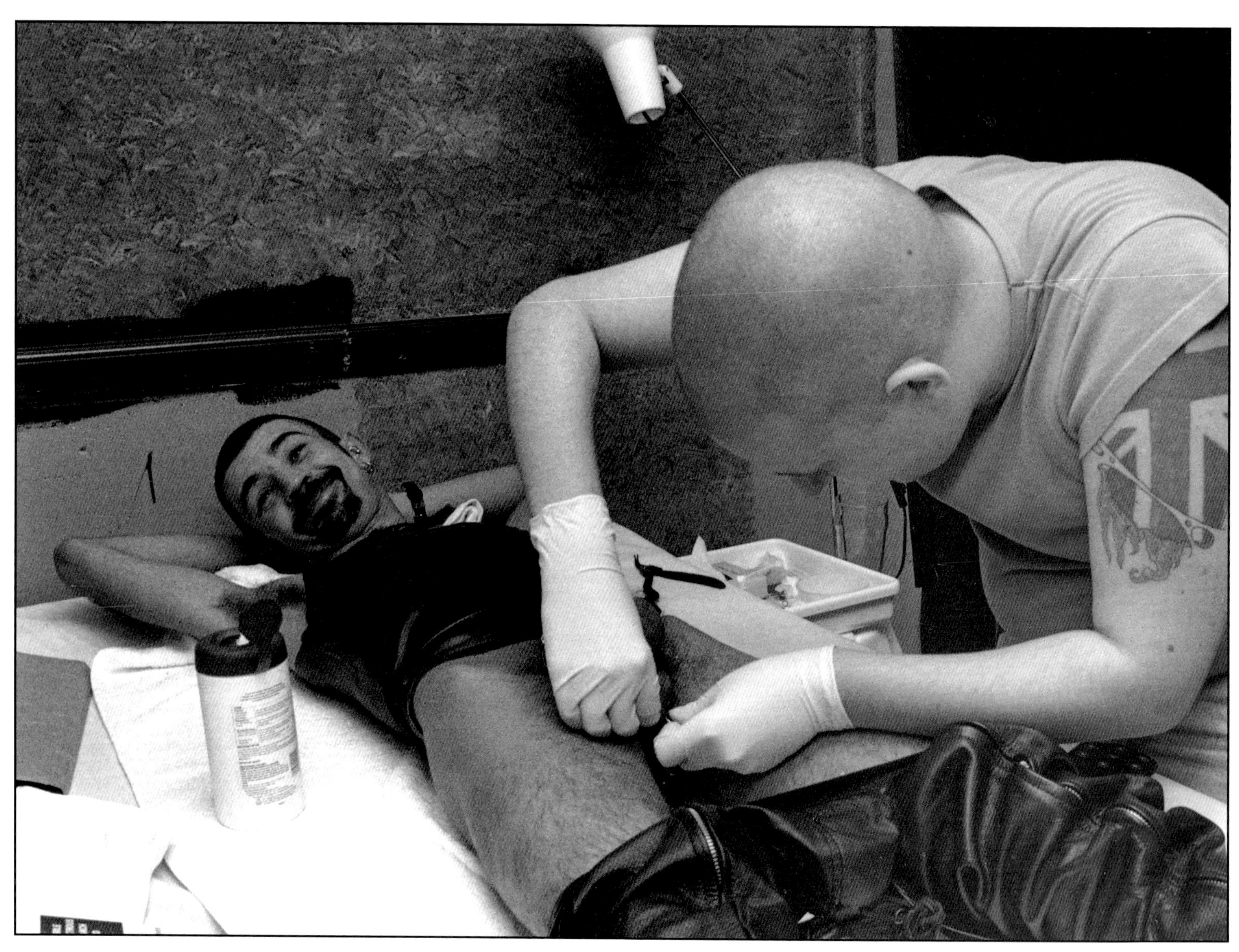

Body Piercing.

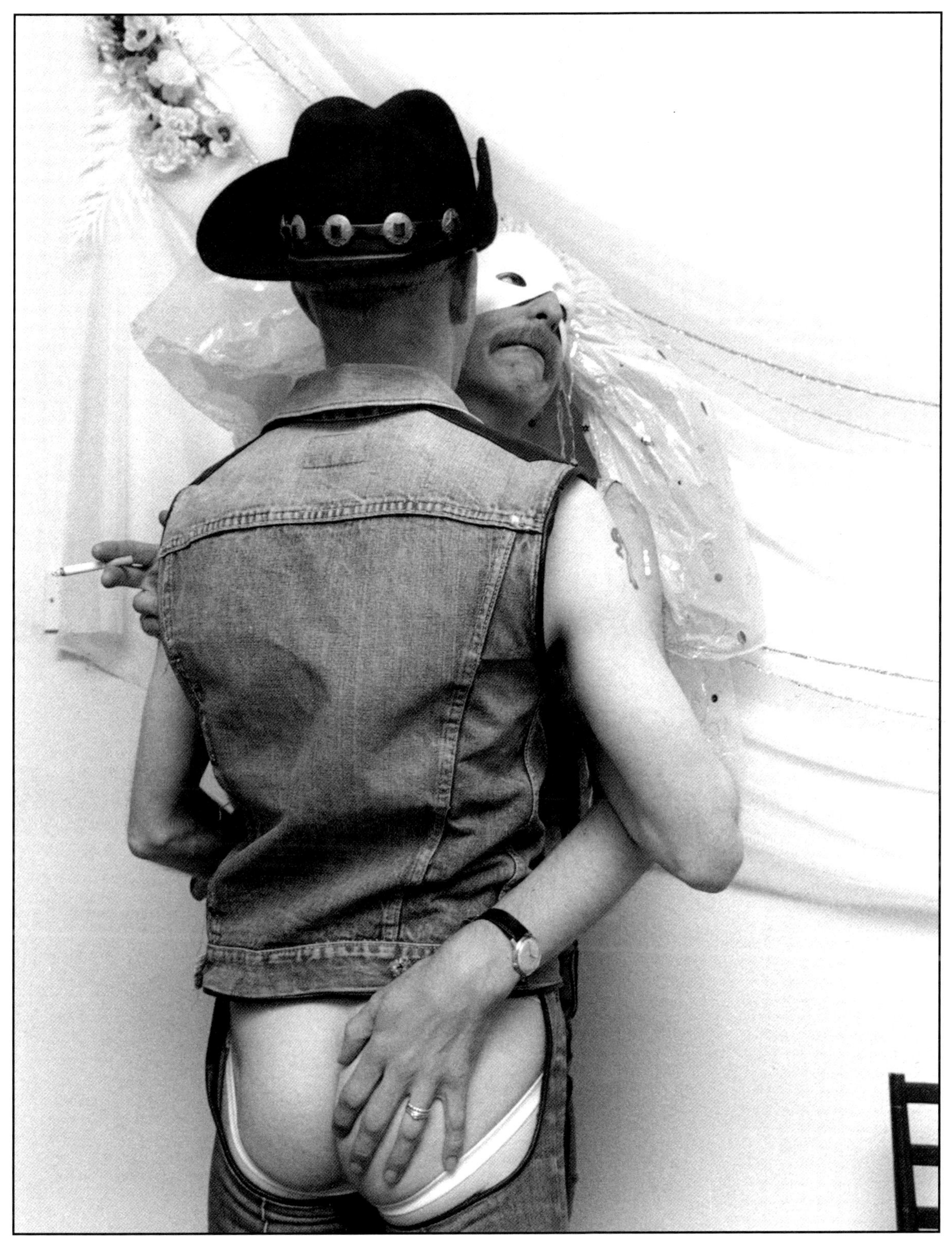

WORKMEN.

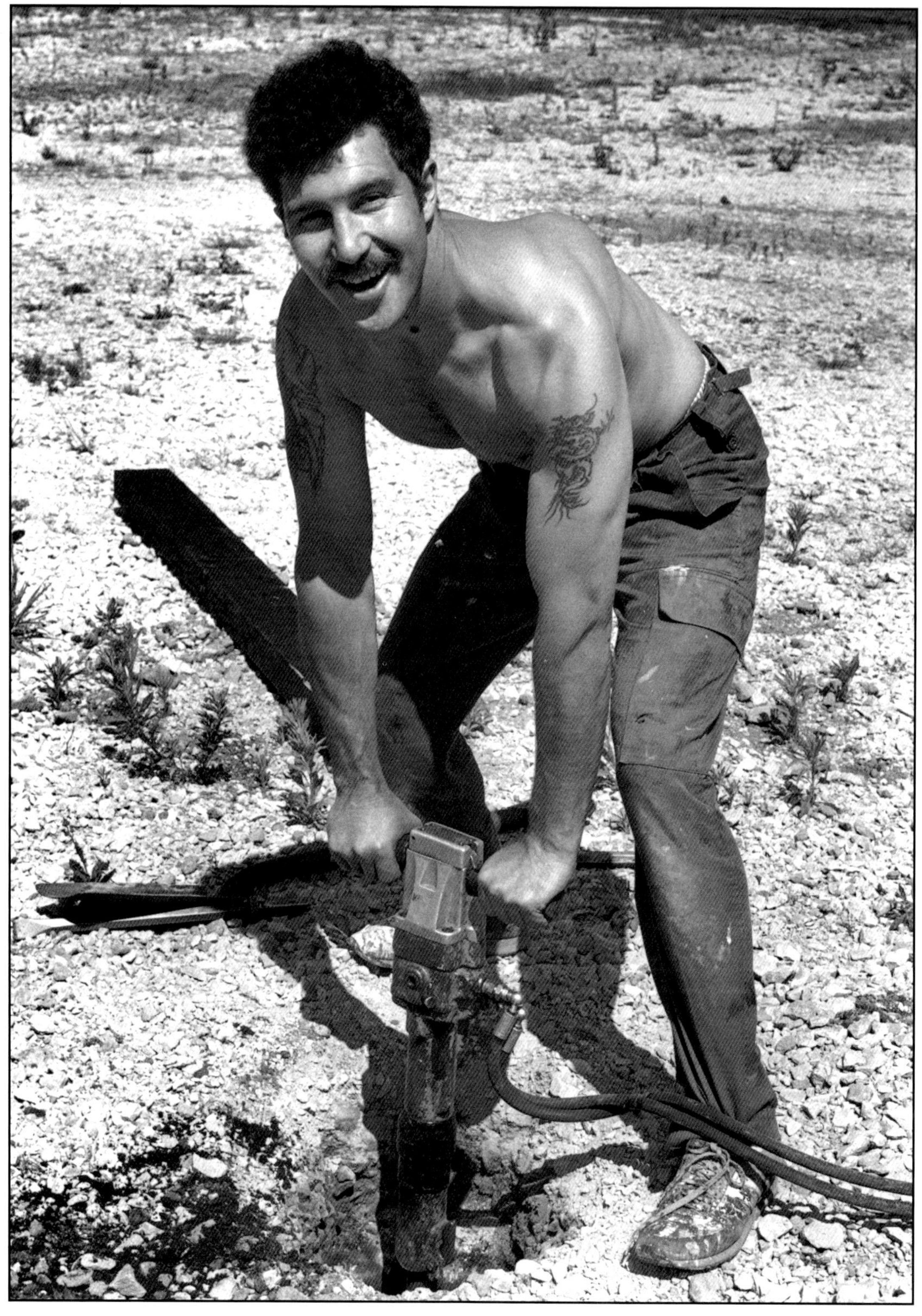

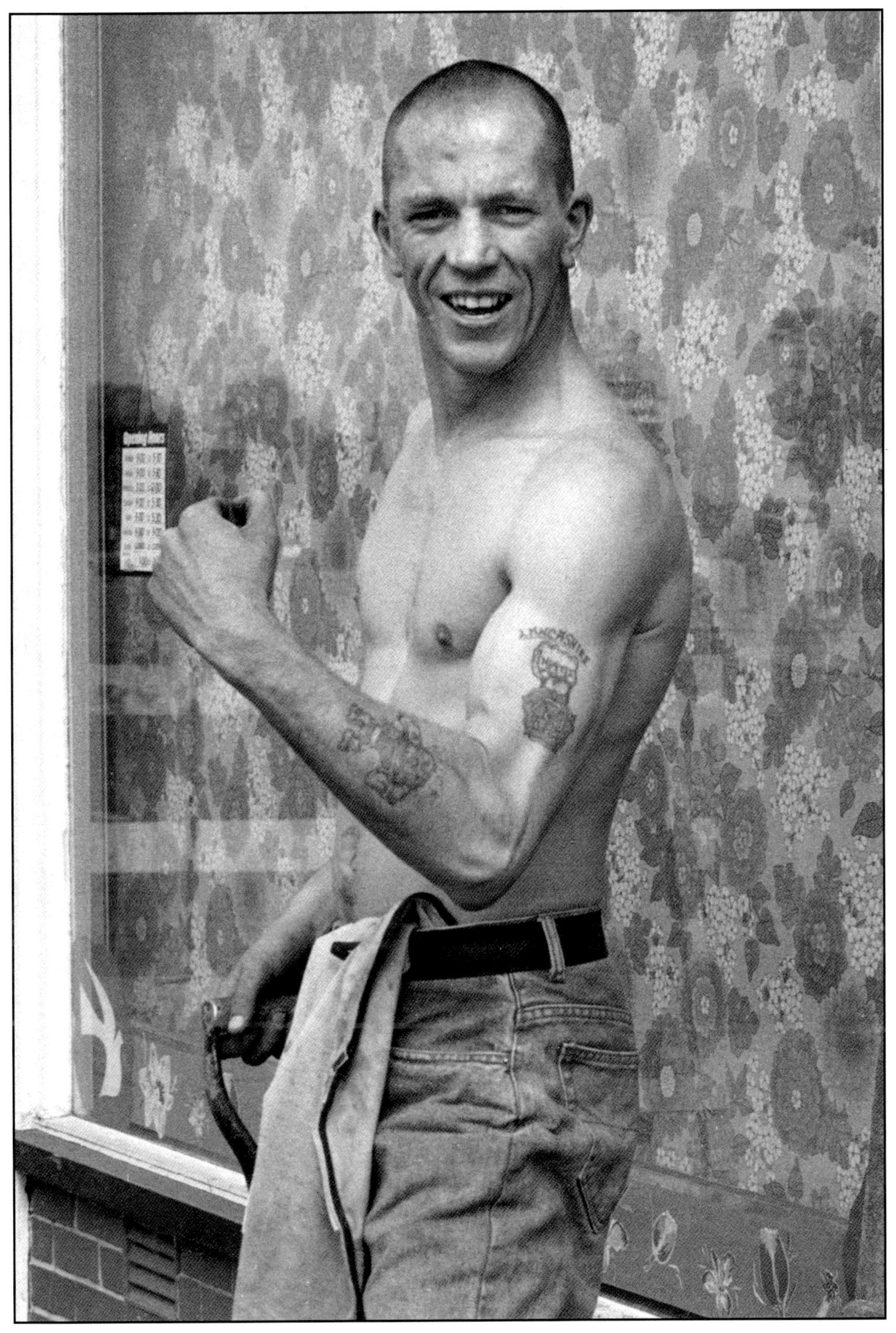

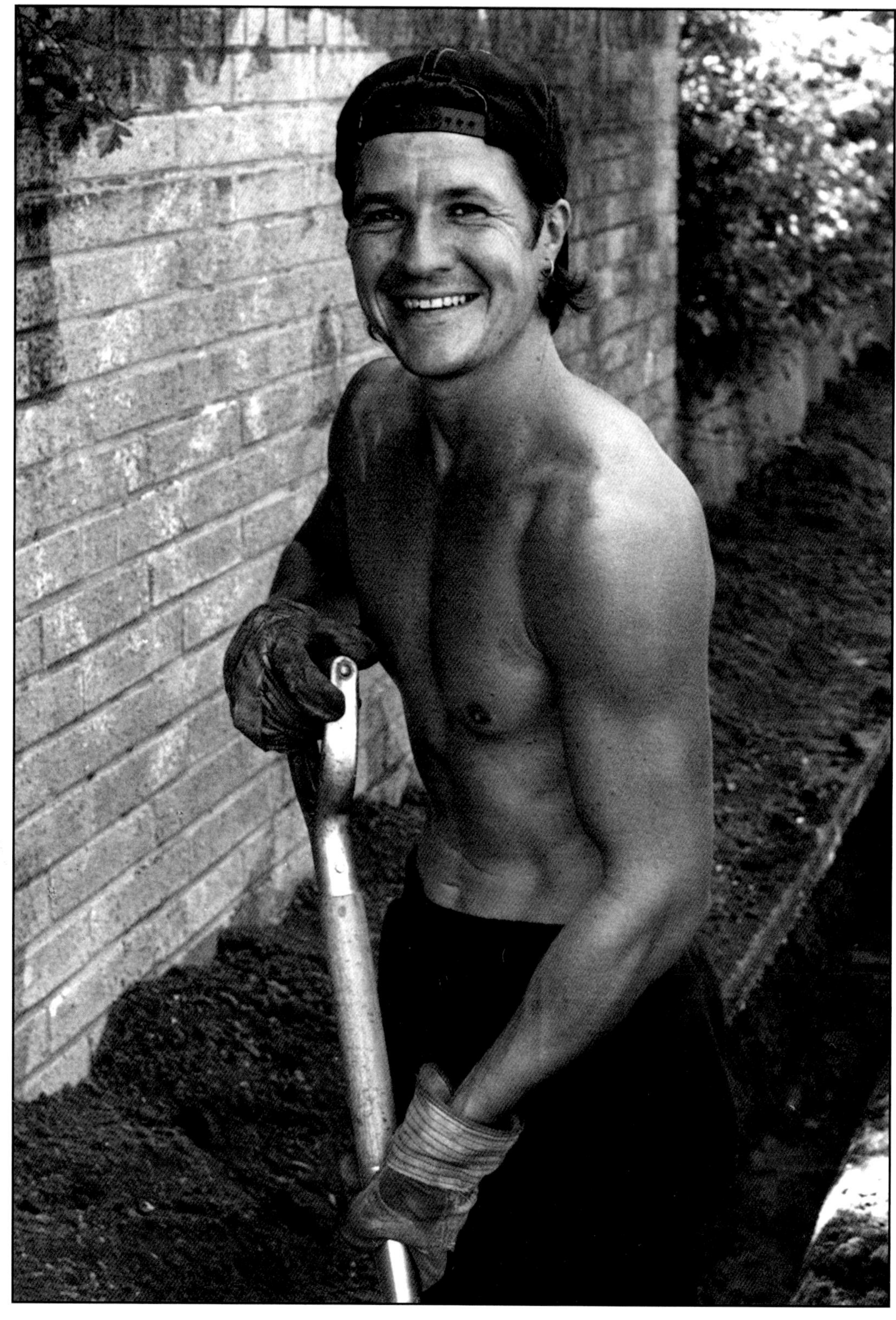

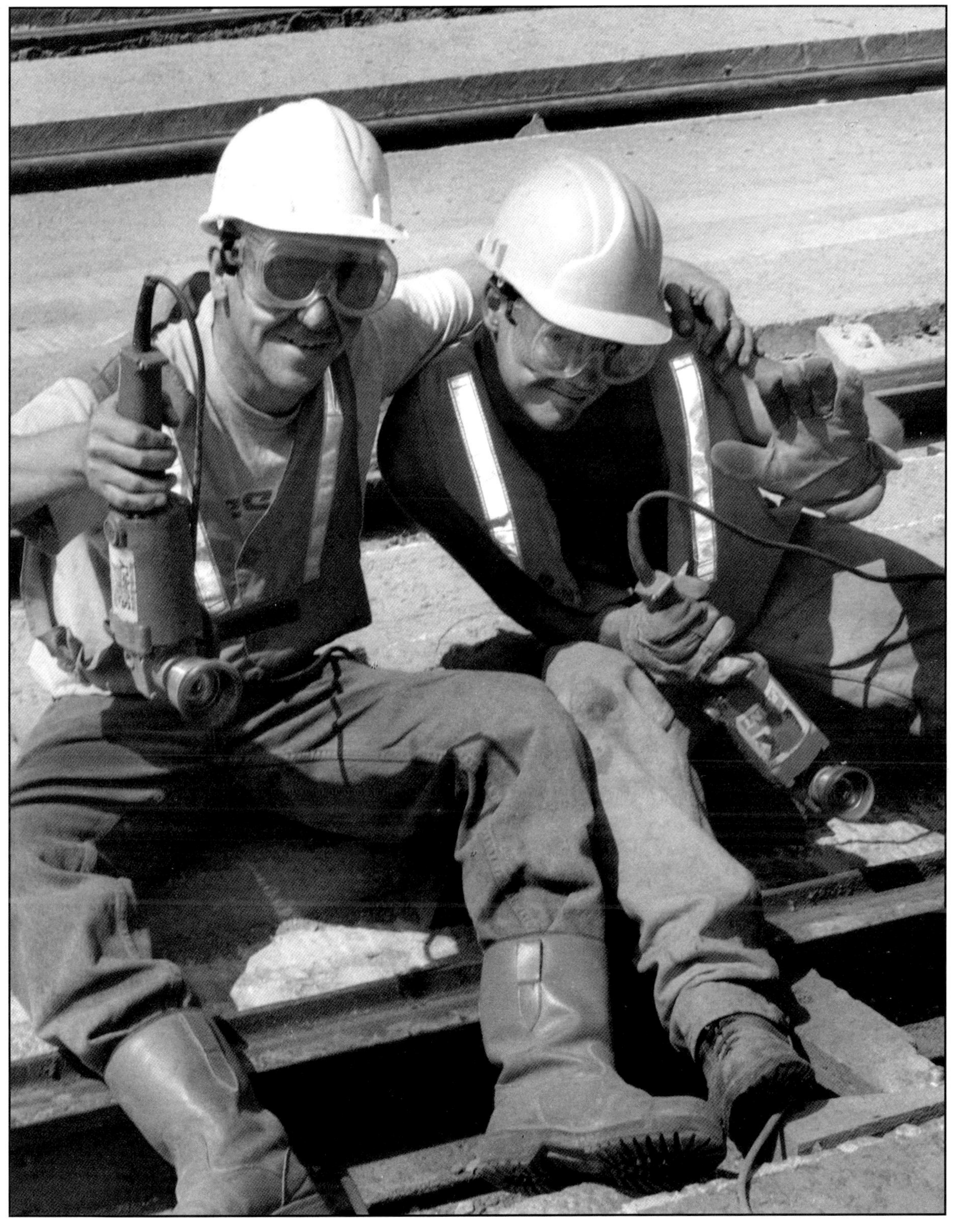

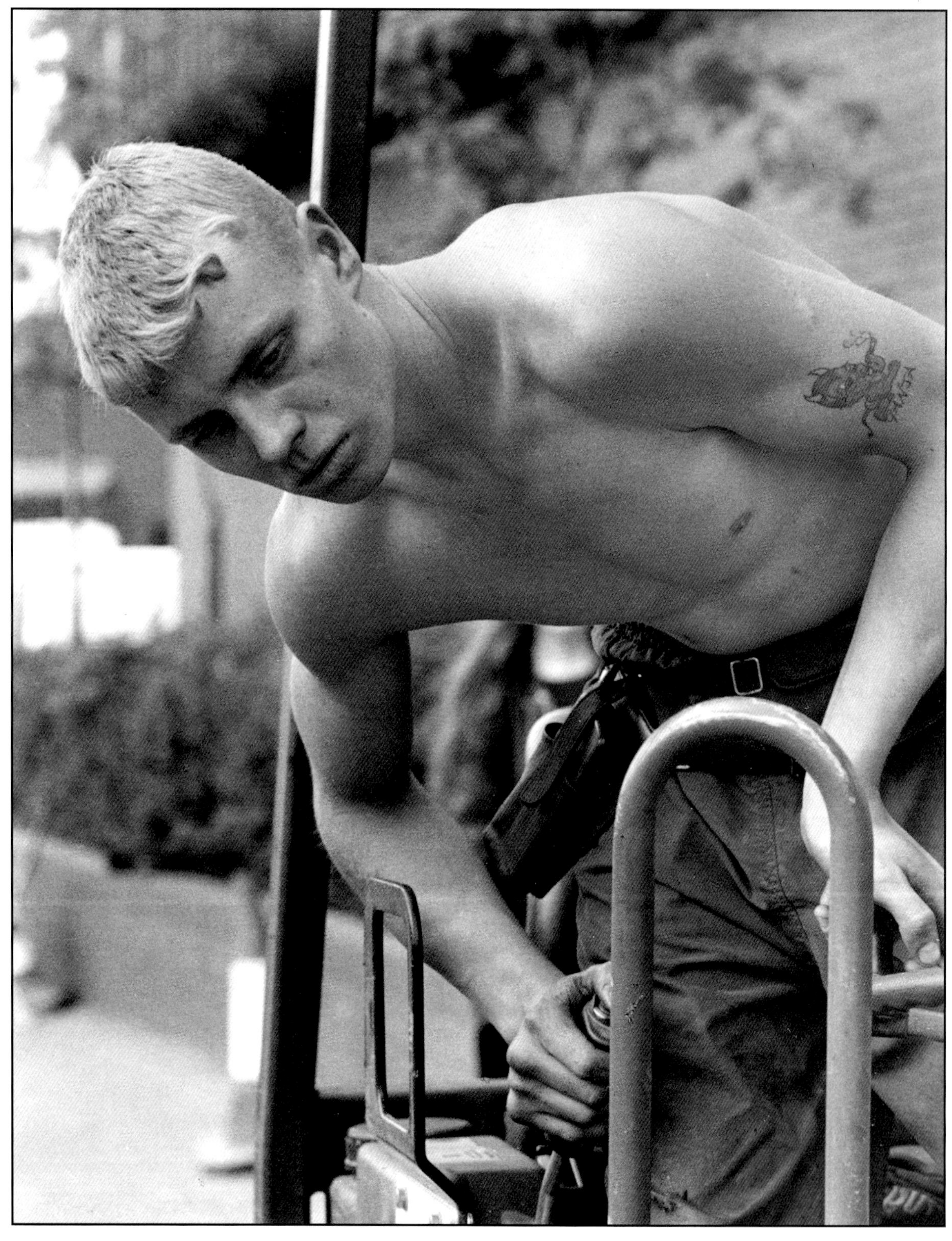

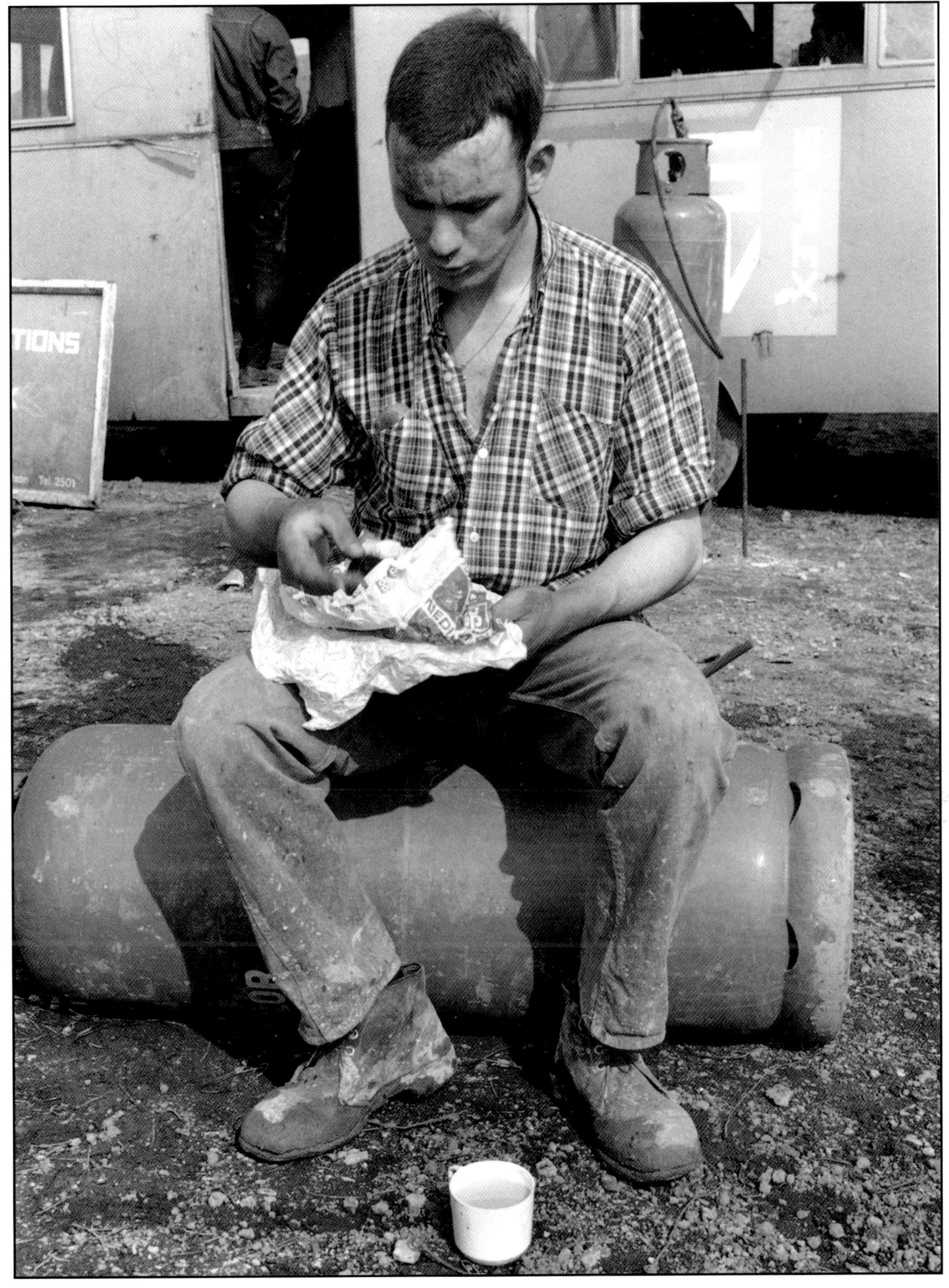

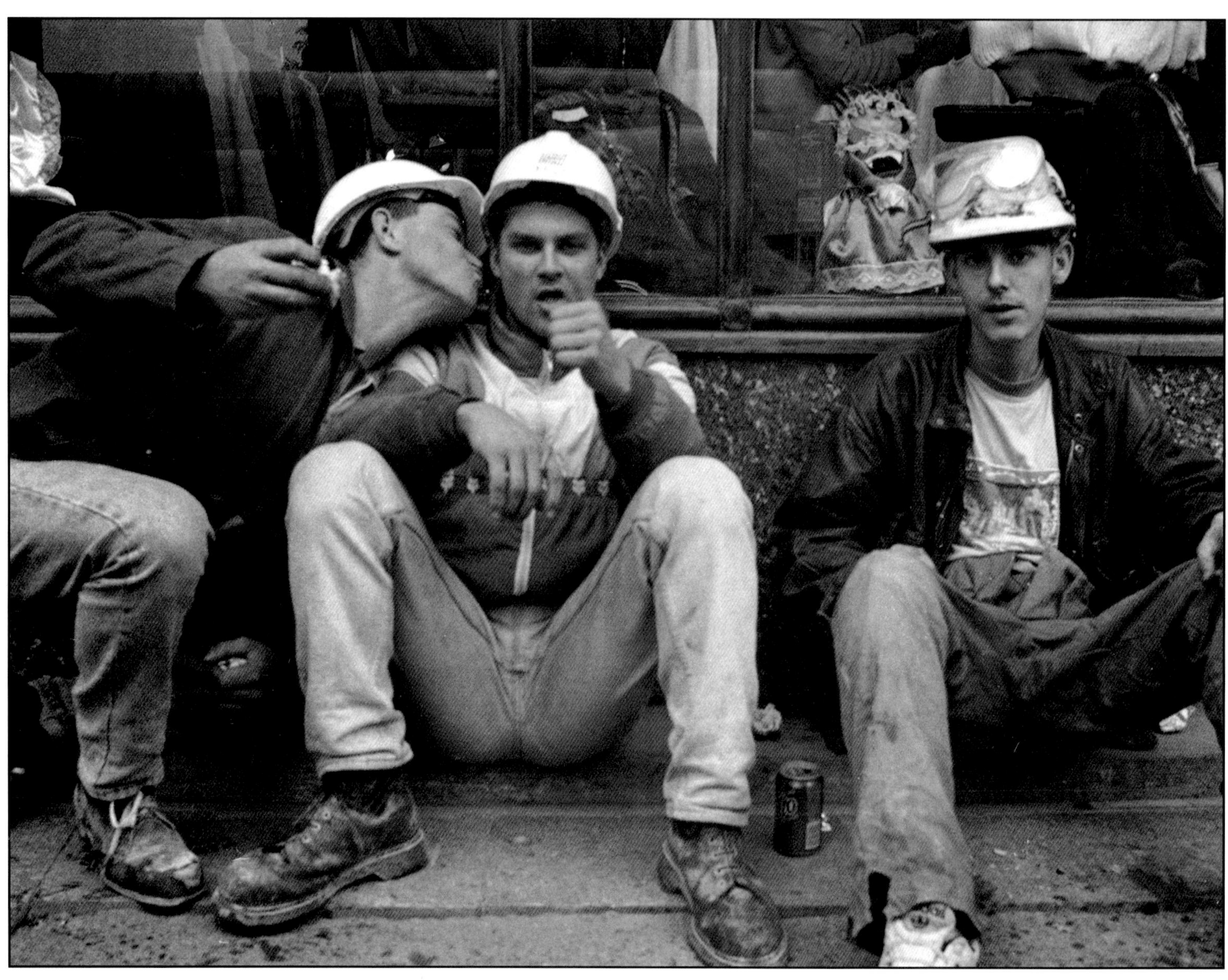

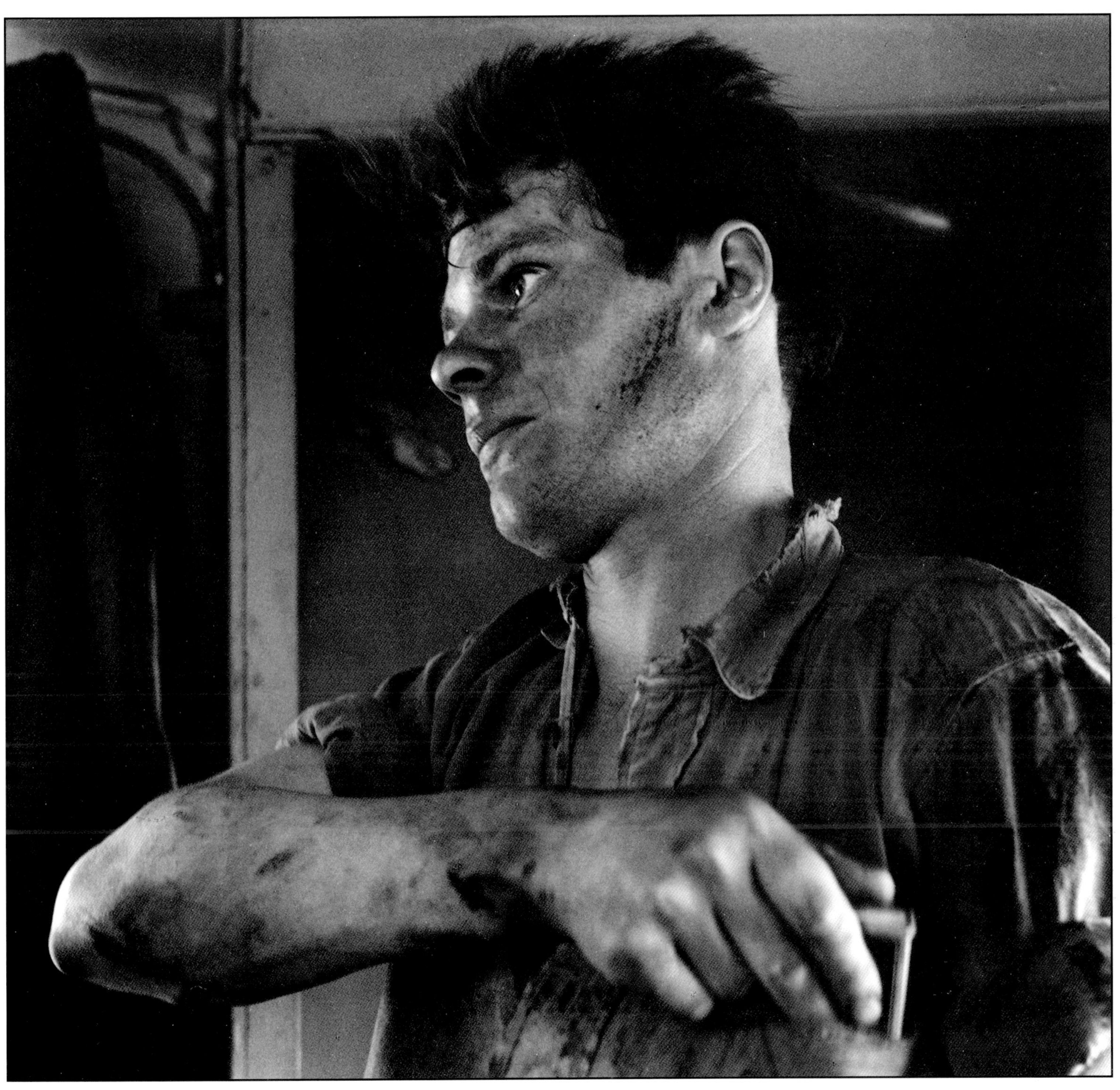

OUT AND ABOUT

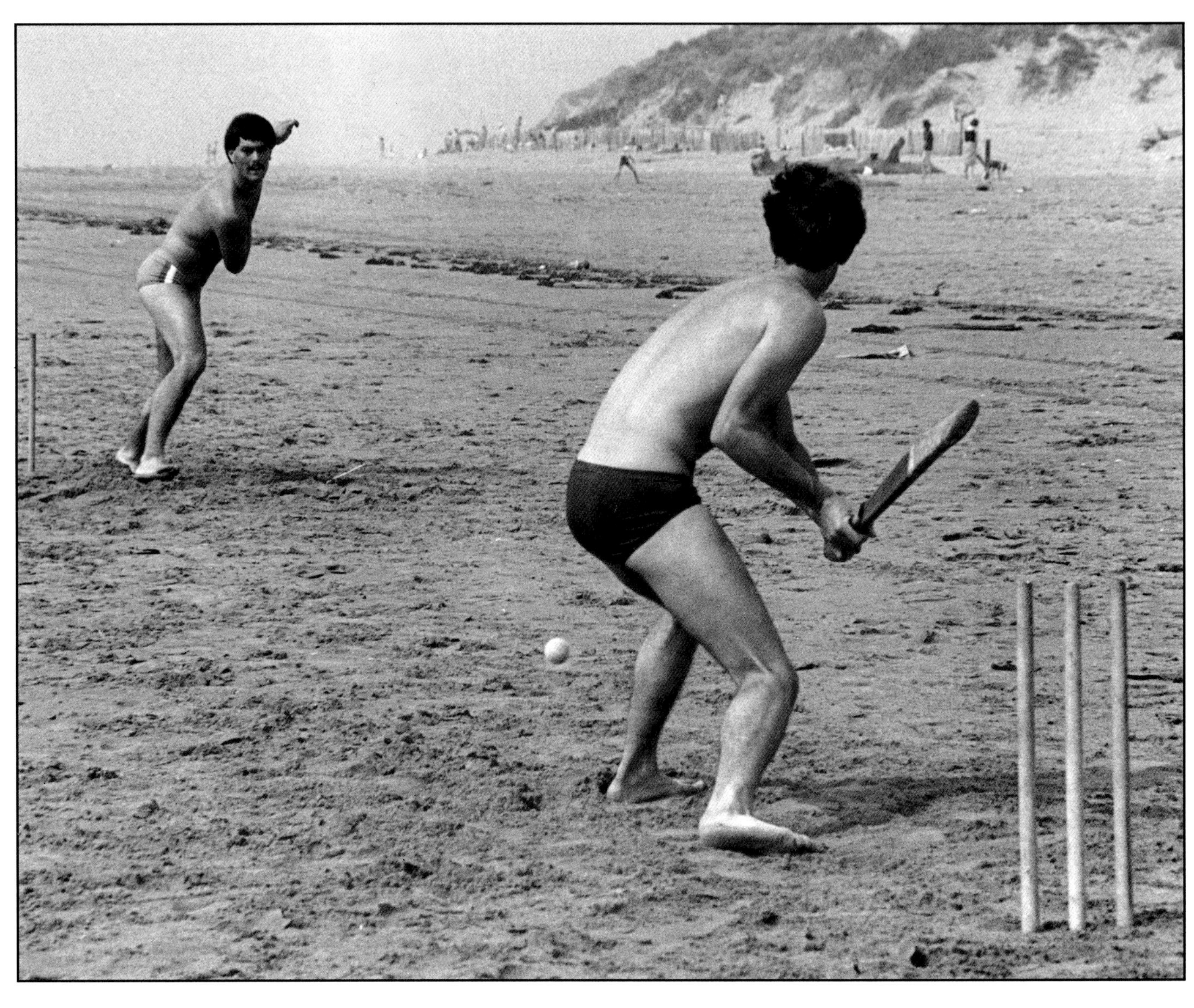

Beach Cricket.

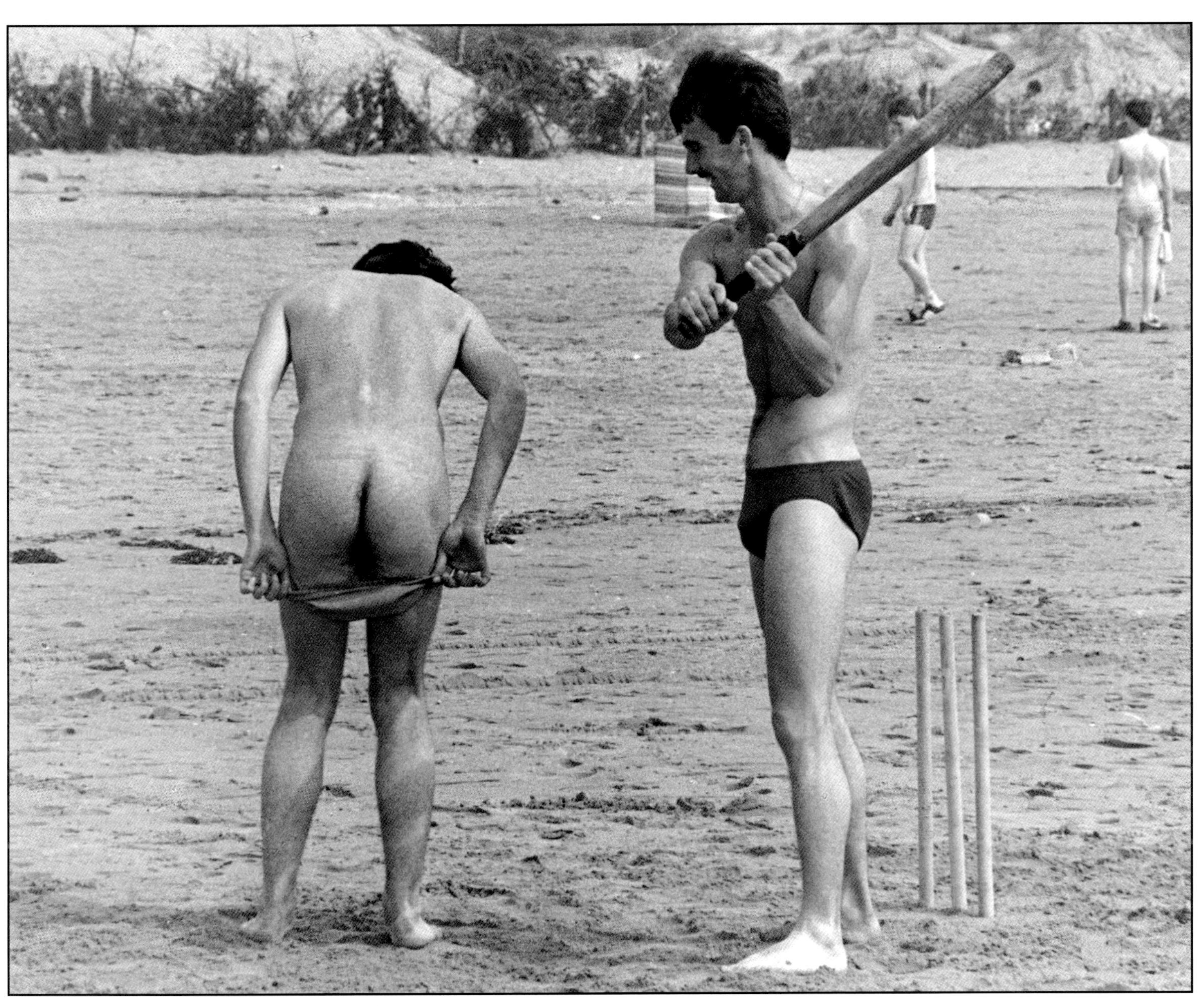

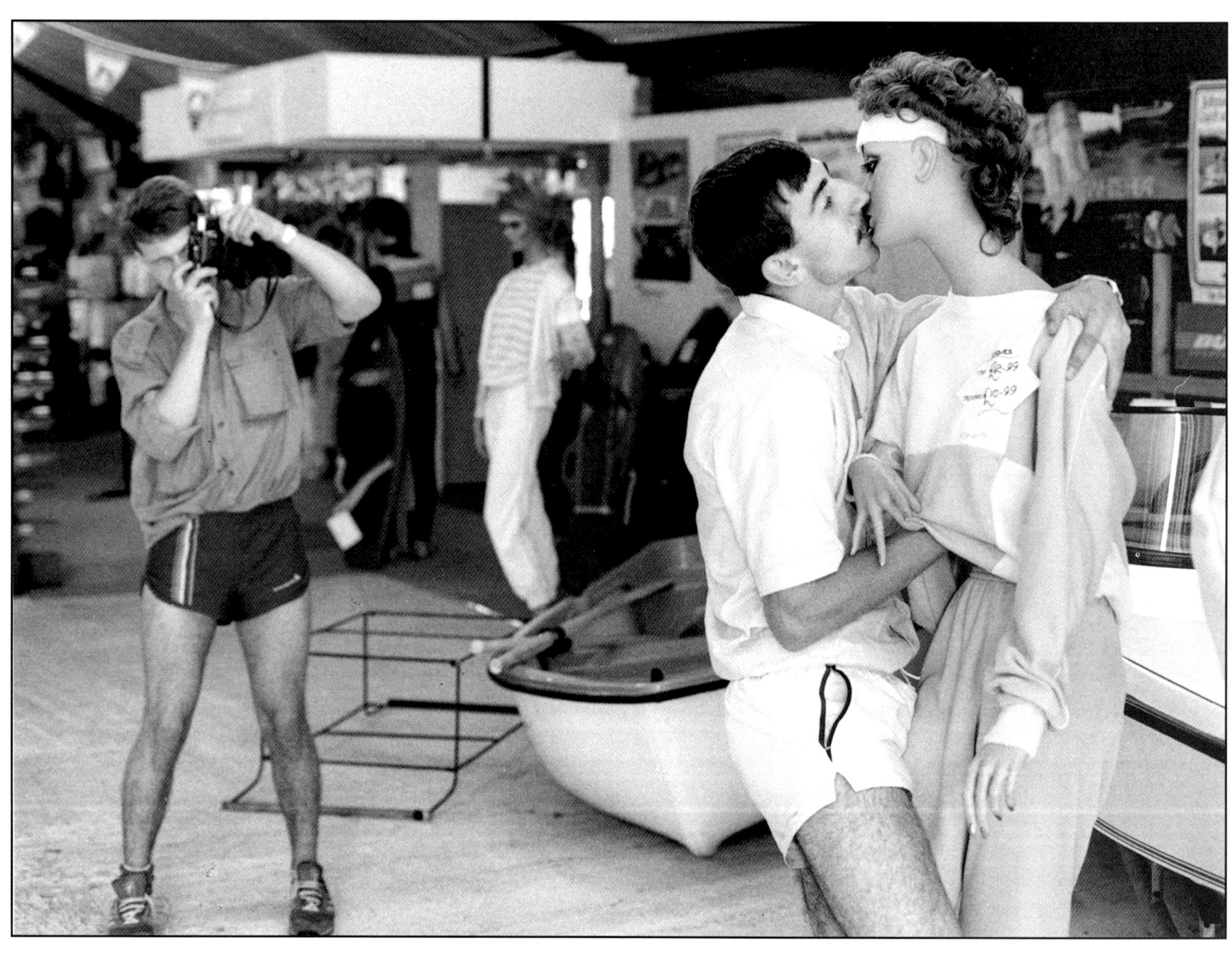

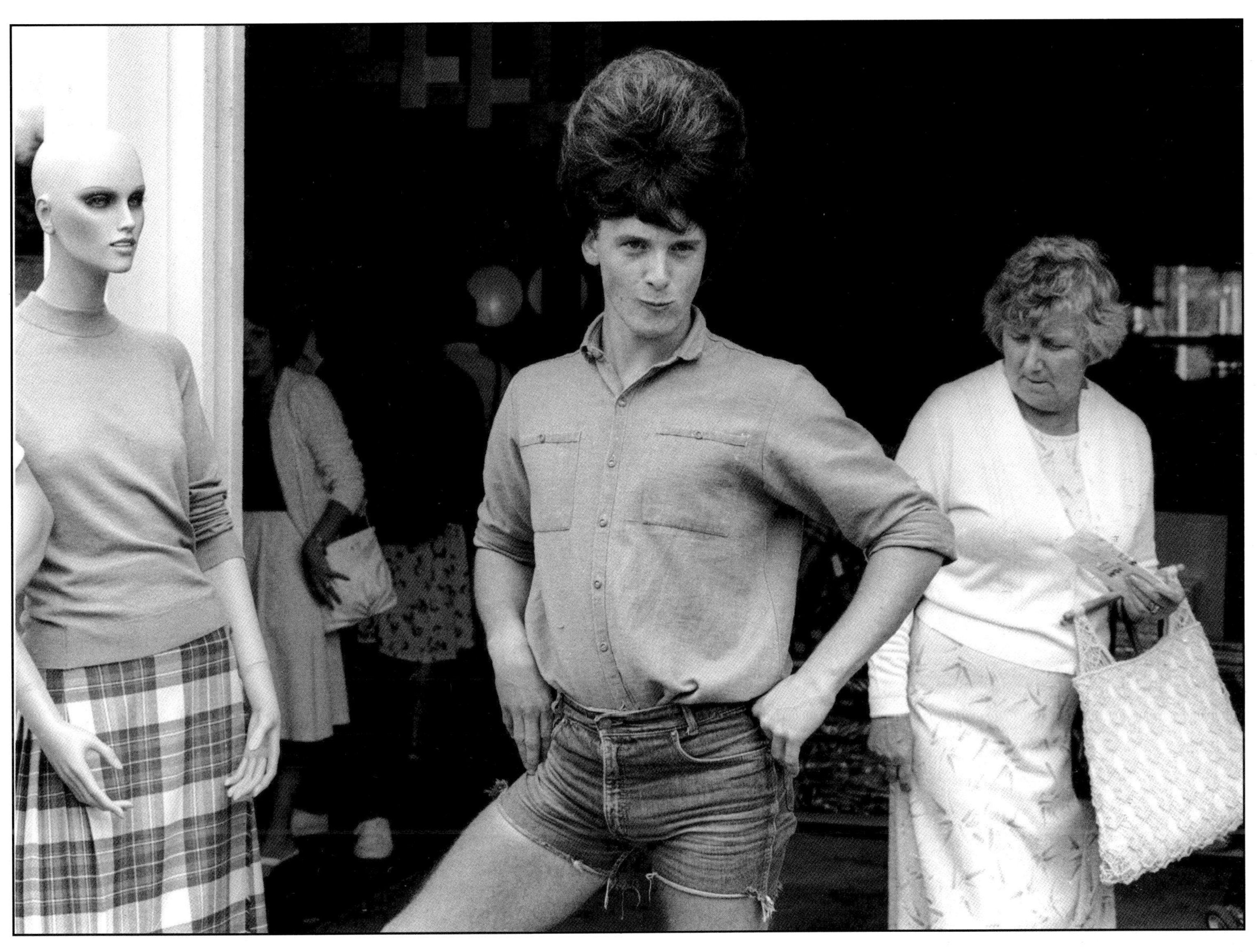

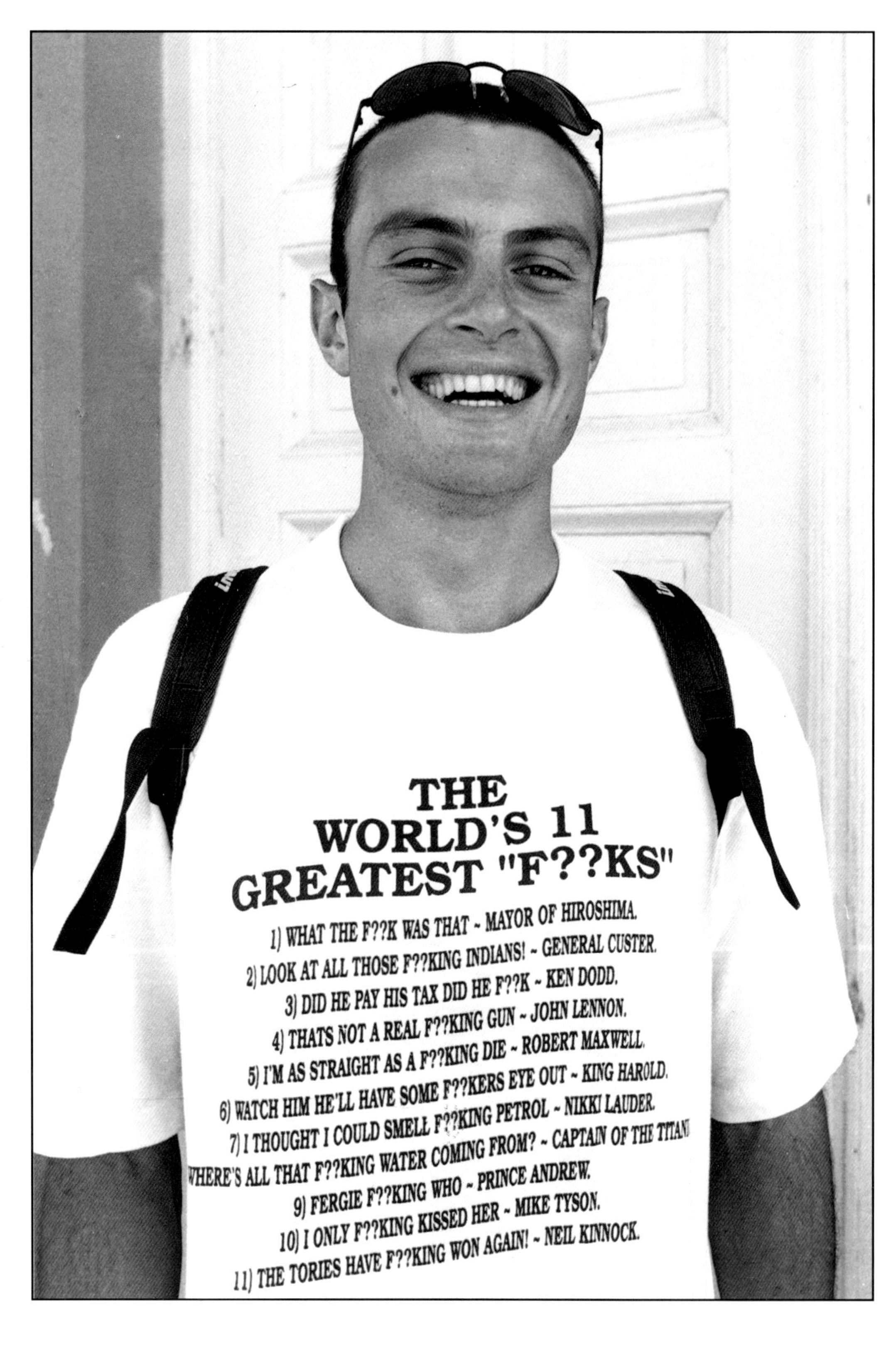
THE
WORLD'S 11
GREATEST "F??KS"
1) WHAT THE F??K WAS THAT ~ MAYOR OF HIROSHIMA.
2) LOOK AT ALL THOSE F??KING INDIANS! ~ GENERAL CUSTER.
3) DID HE PAY HIS TAX DID HE F??K ~ KEN DODD.
4) THATS NOT A REAL F??KING GUN ~ JOHN LENNON.
5) I'M AS STRAIGHT AS A F??KING DIE ~ ROBERT MAXWELL.
6) WATCH HIM HE'LL HAVE SOME F??KERS EYE OUT ~ KING HAROLD.
7) I THOUGHT I COULD SMELL F??KING PETROL ~ NIKKI LAUDER.
WHERE'S ALL THAT F??KING WATER COMING FROM? ~ CAPTAIN OF THE TITANI
9) FERGIE F??KING WHO ~ PRINCE ANDREW.
10) I ONLY F??KING KISSED HER ~ MIKE TYSON.
11) THE TORIES HAVE F??KING WON AGAIN! ~ NEIL KINNOCK.

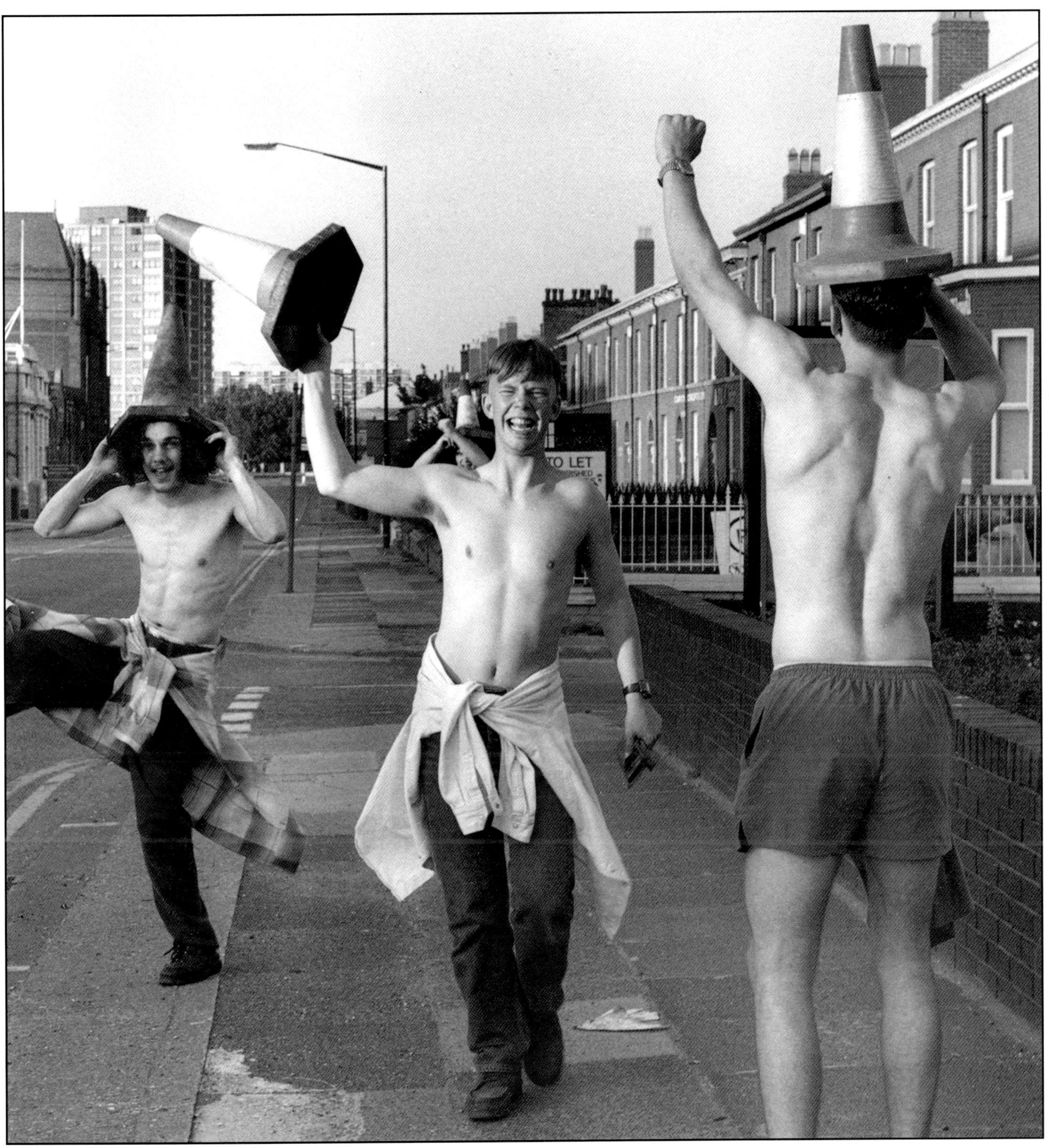

TO LET
FURNISHED

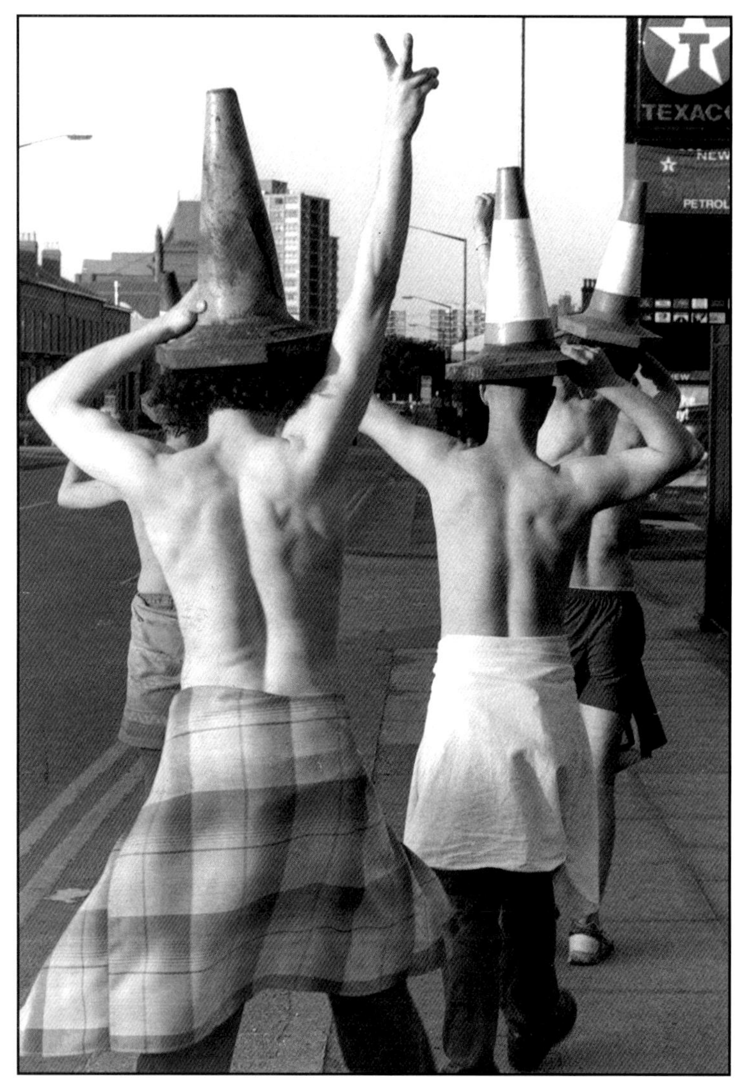

TEXACO
NEW
PETROL

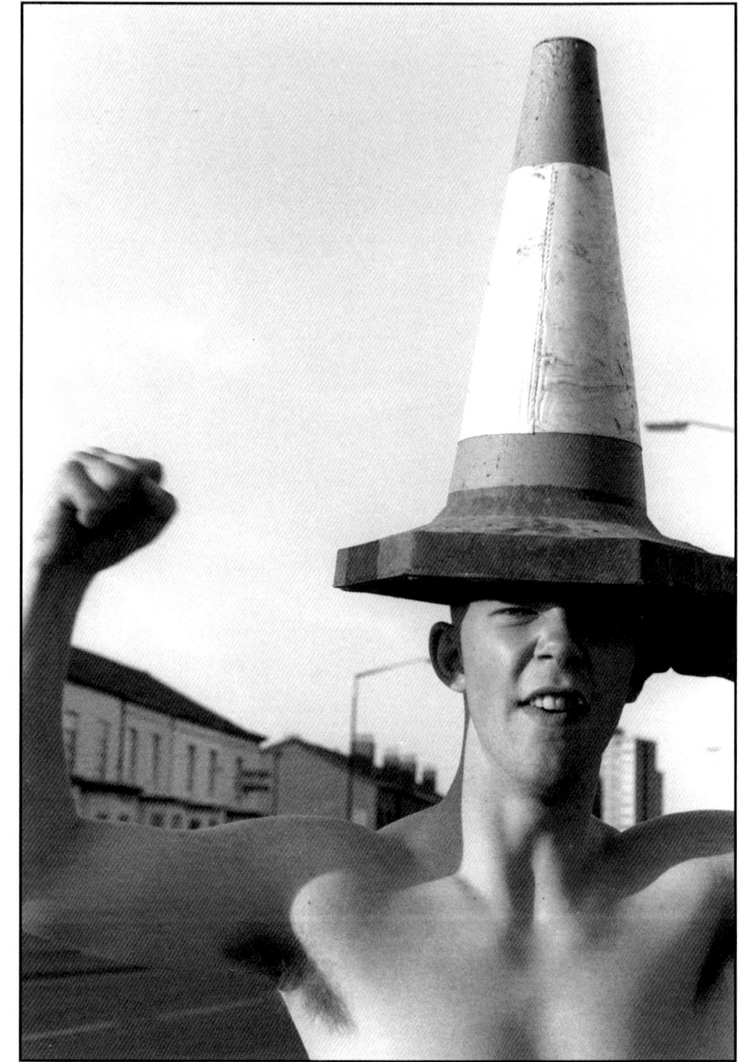

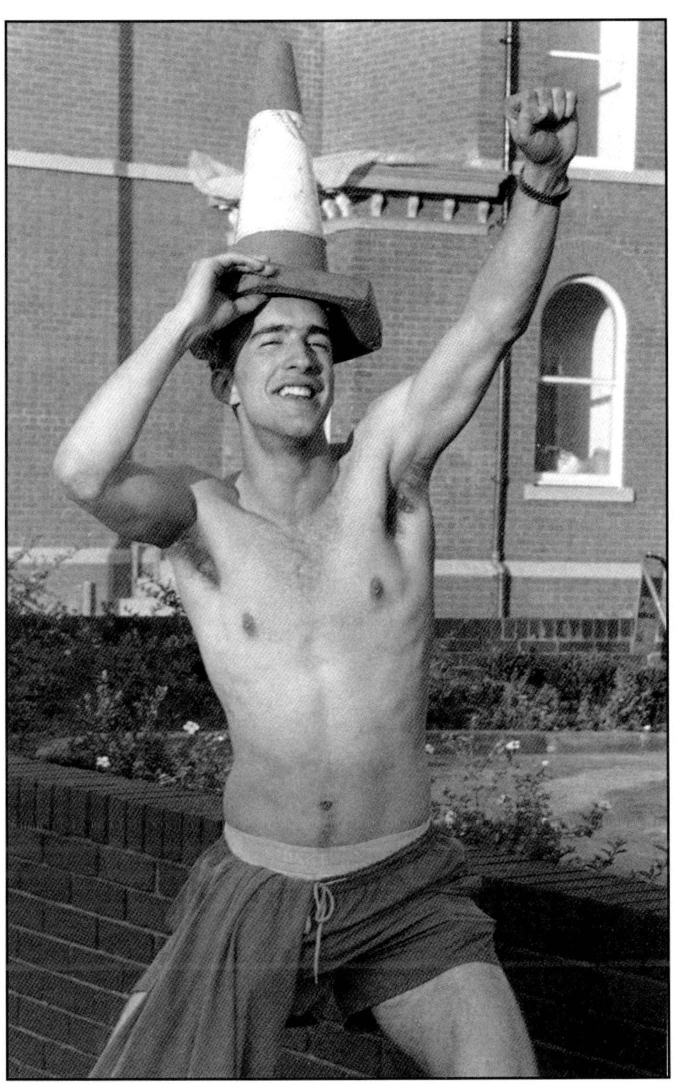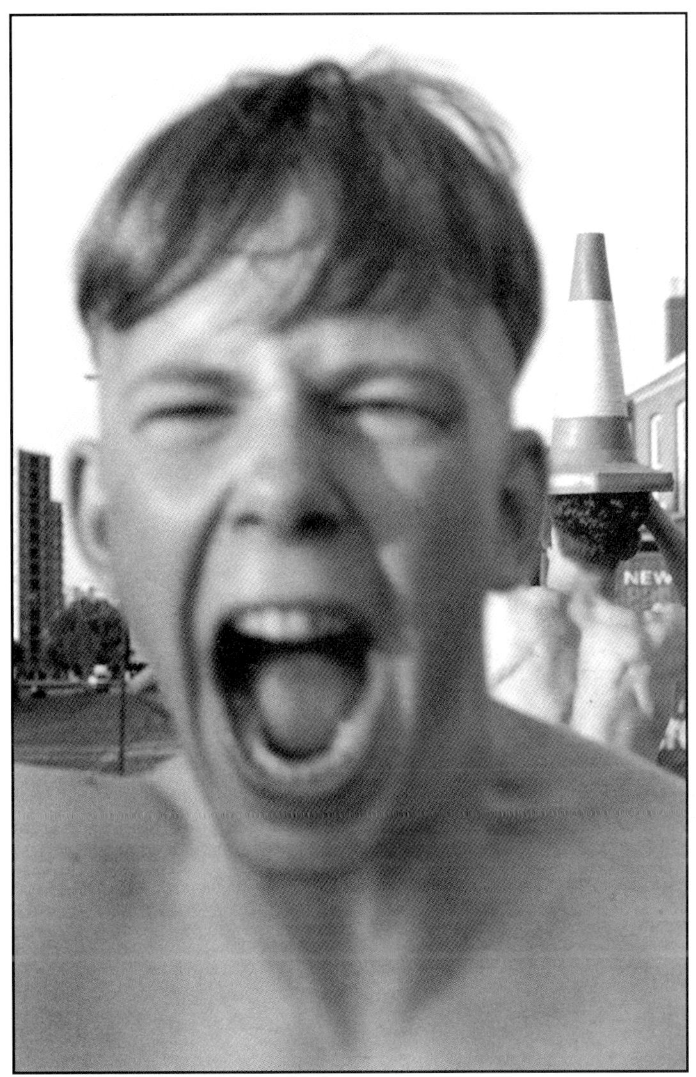

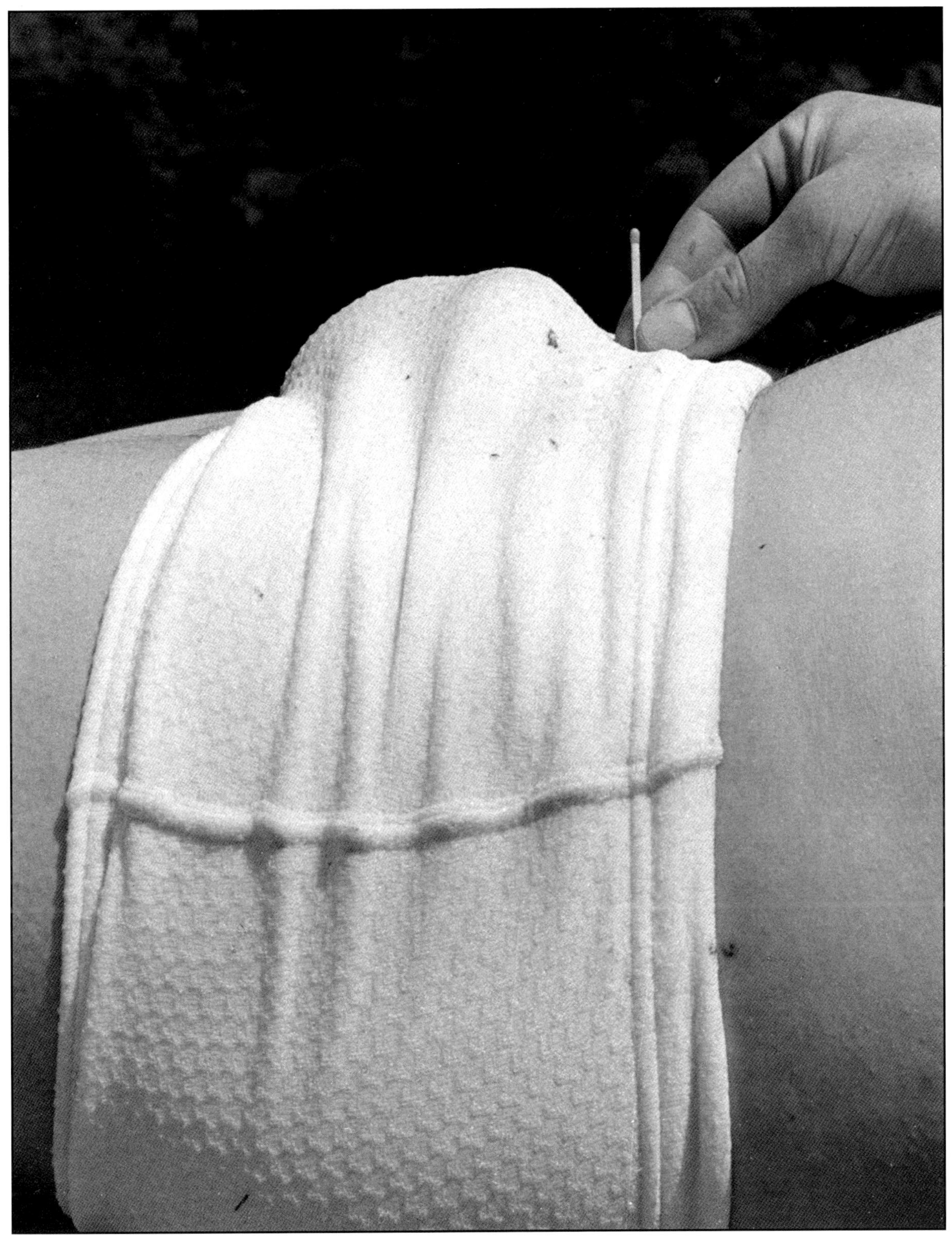

Measuring up.

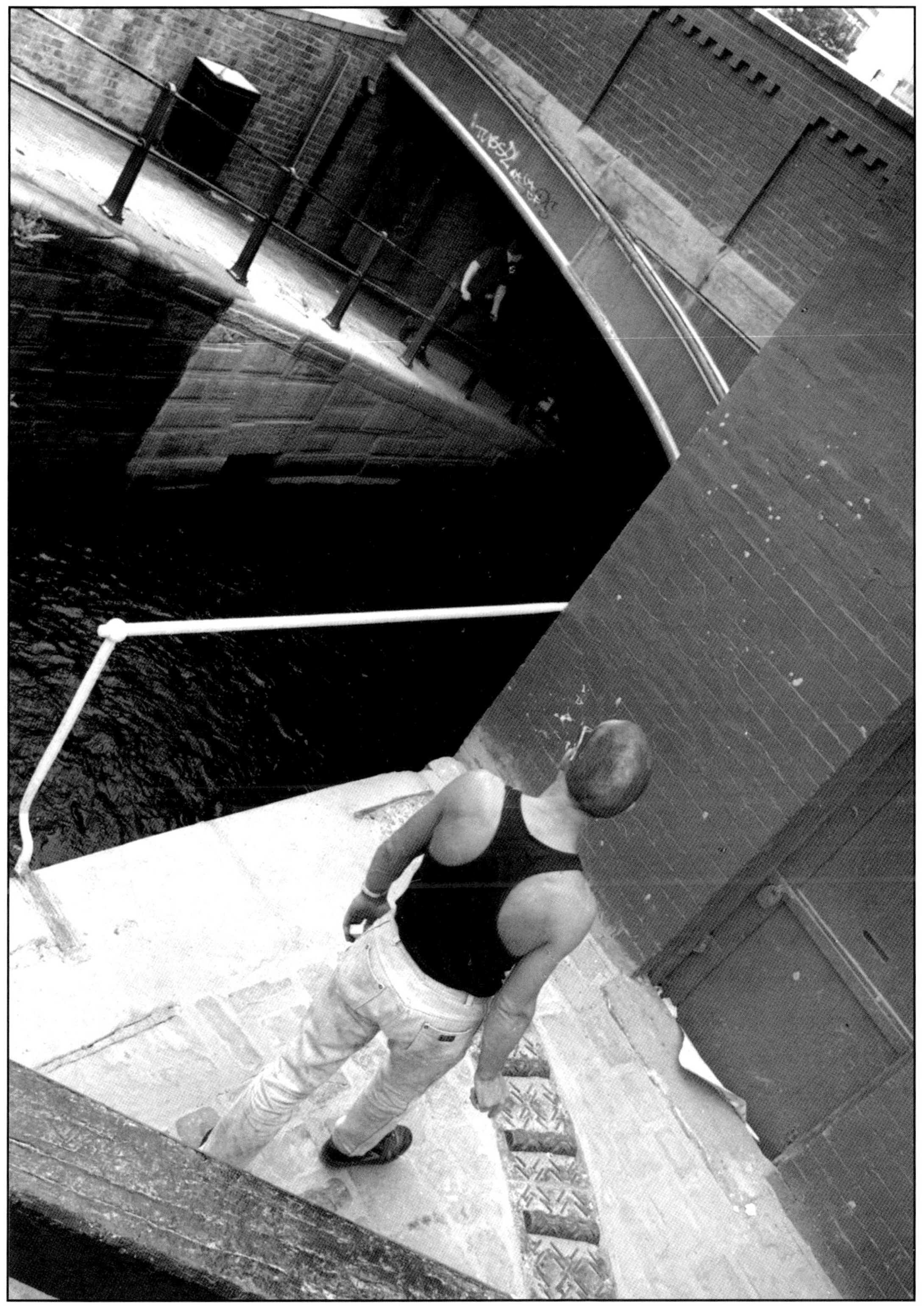

LOCKER ROOMS.

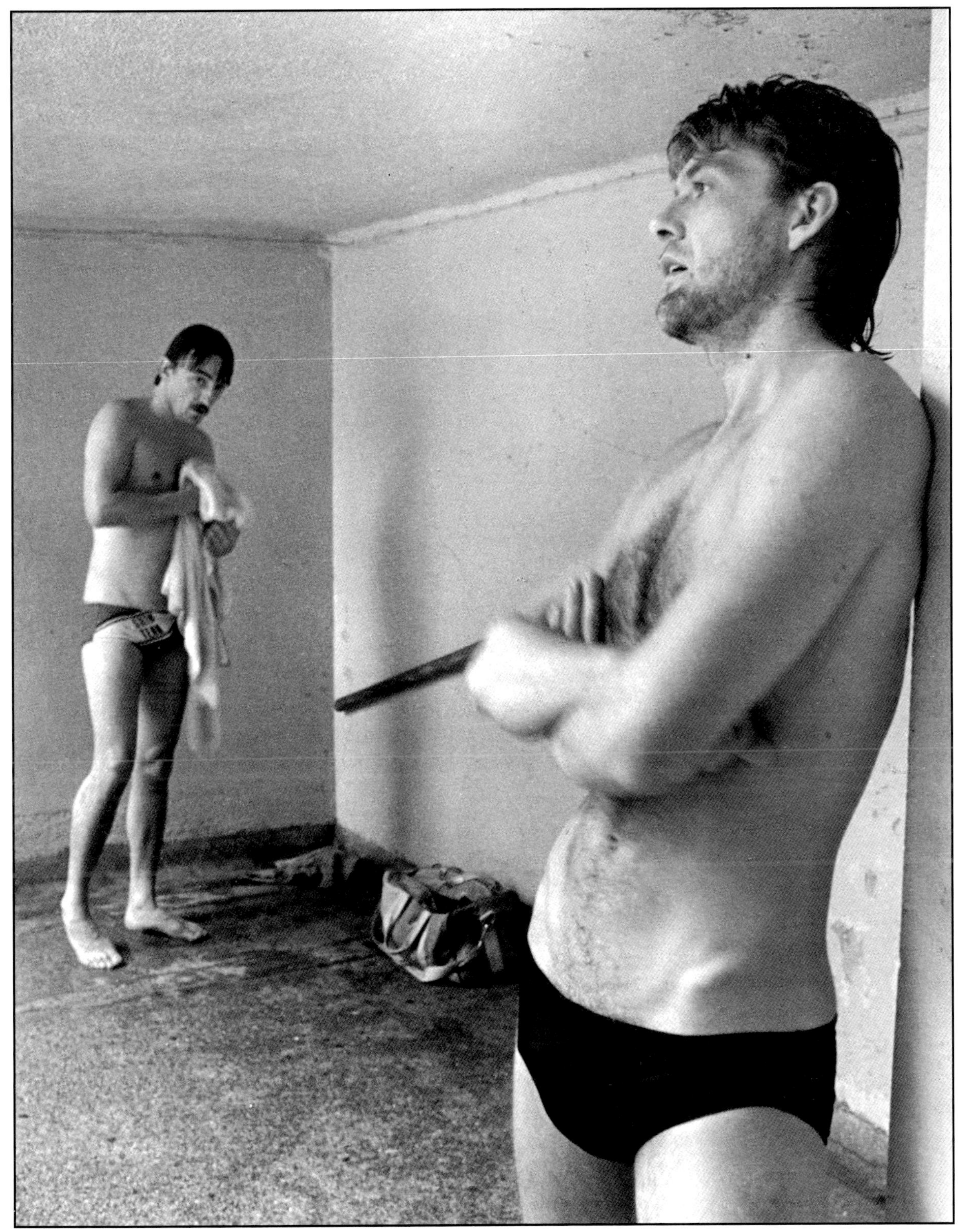

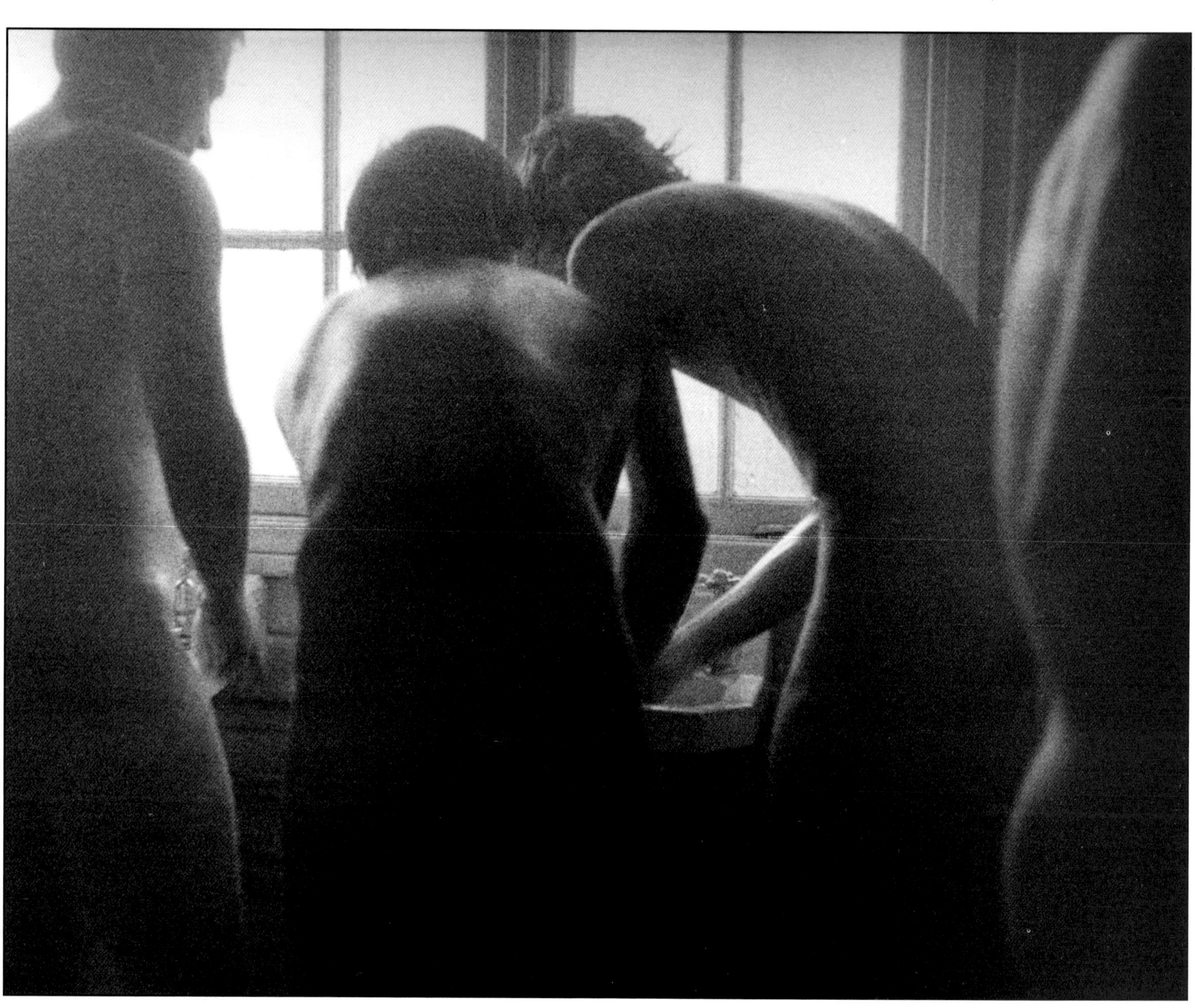

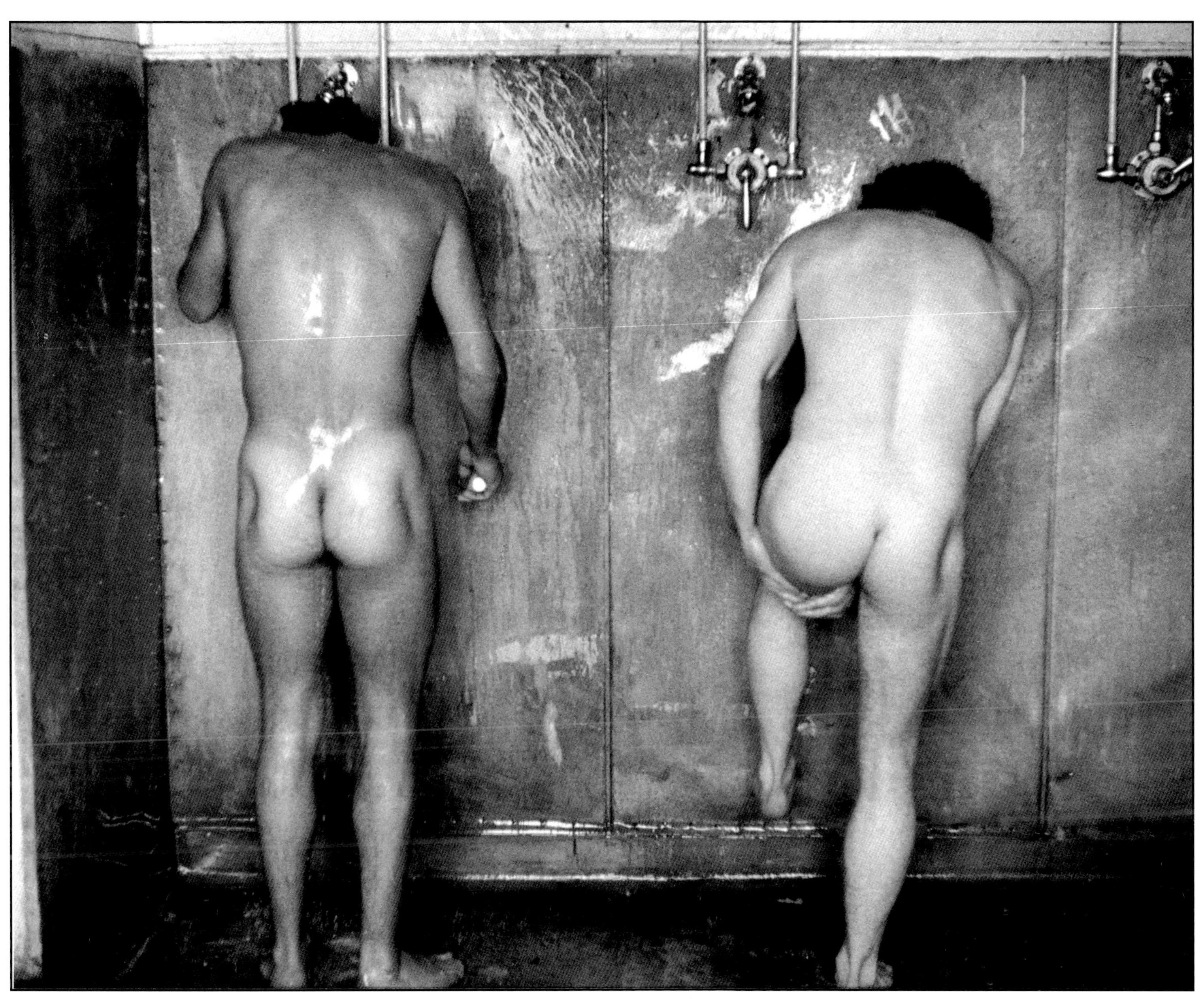

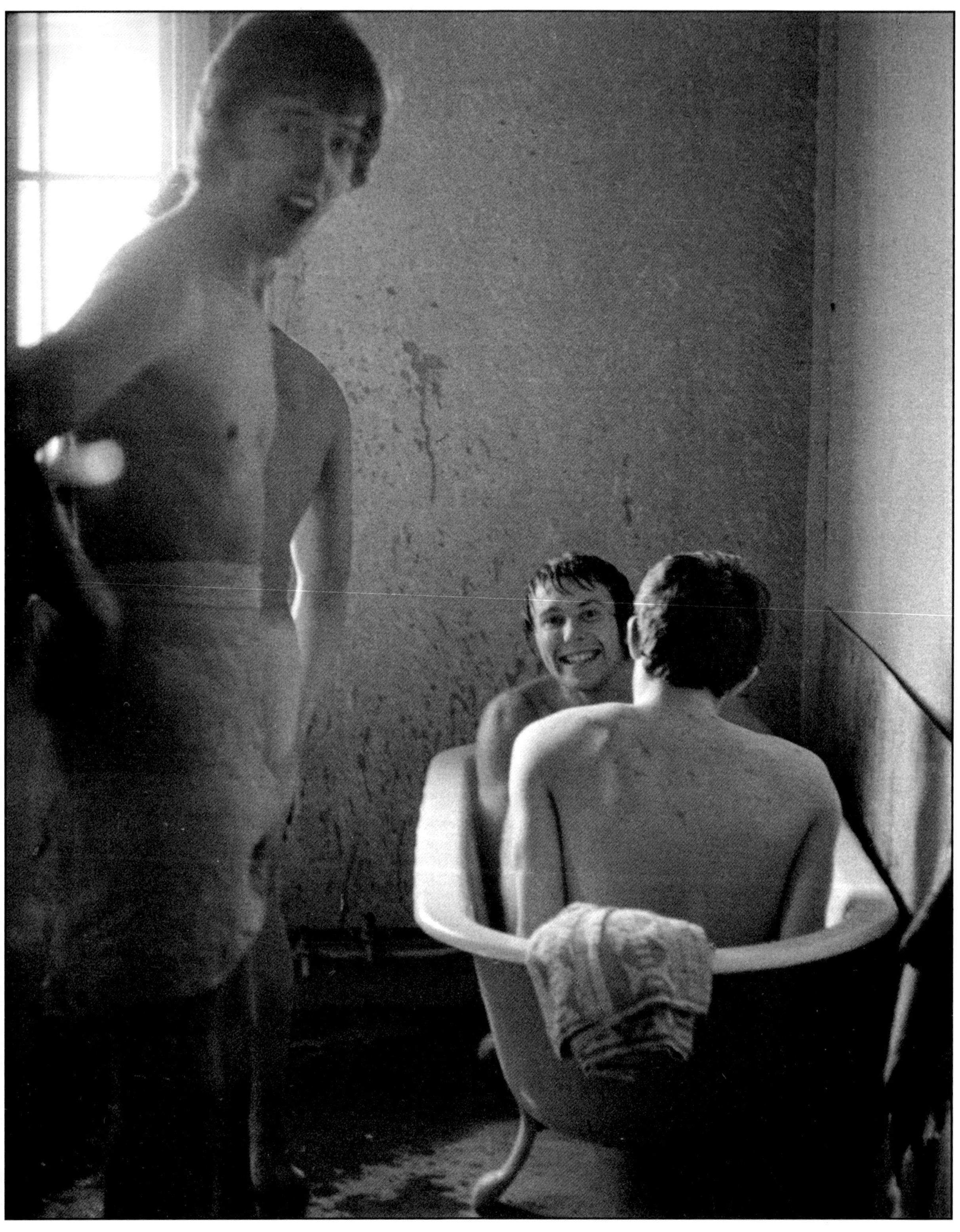

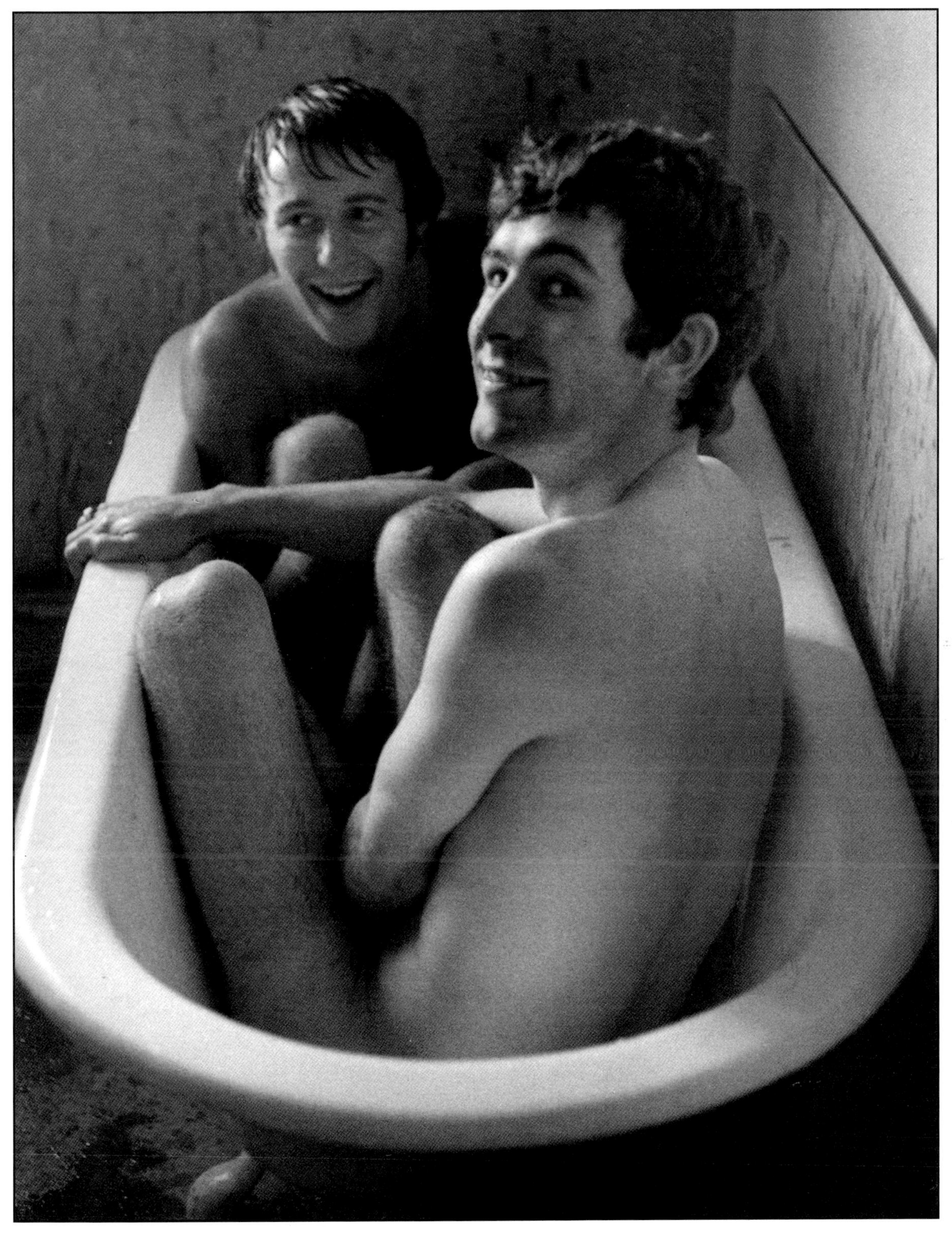

MEN POSING.

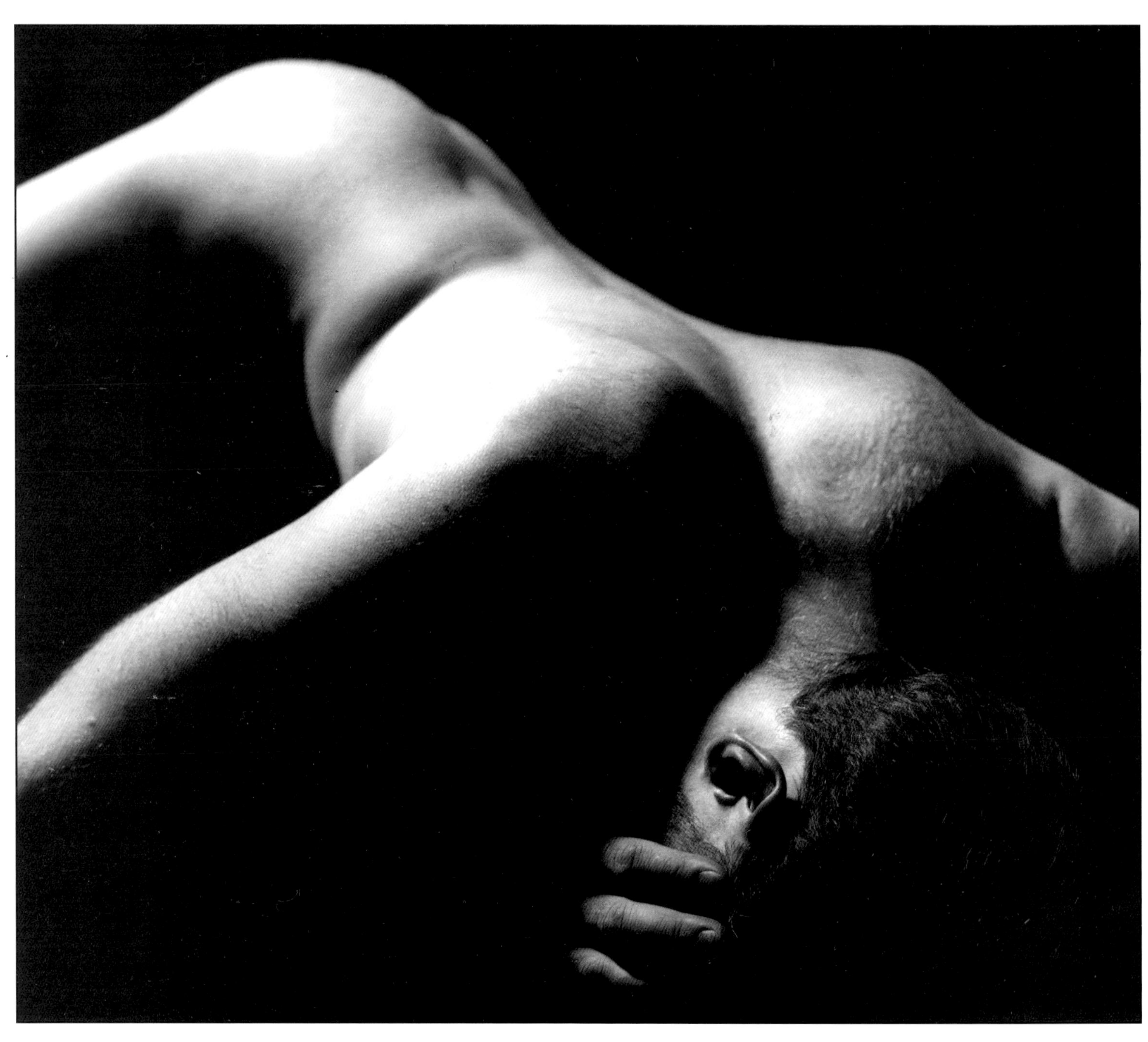

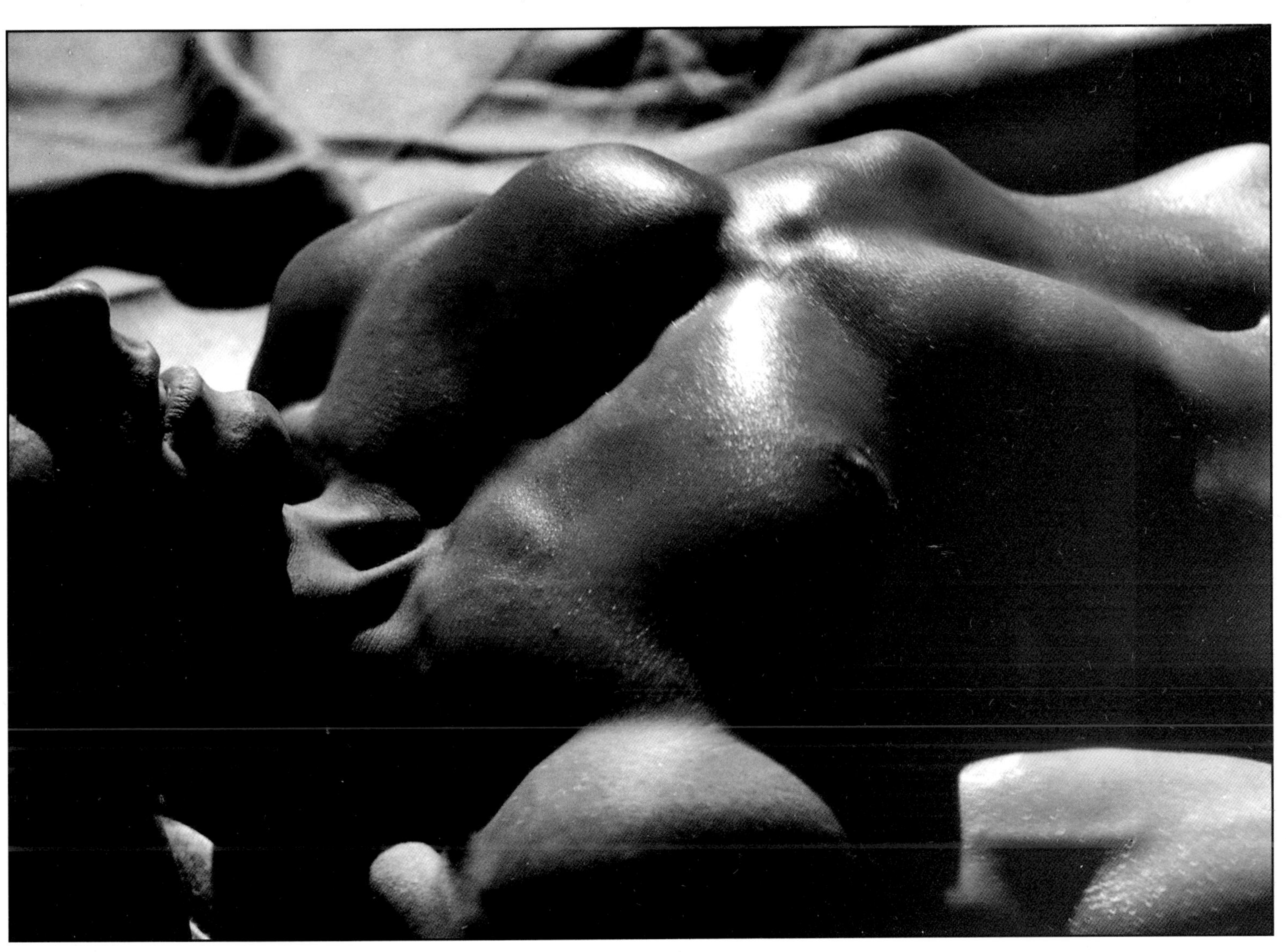

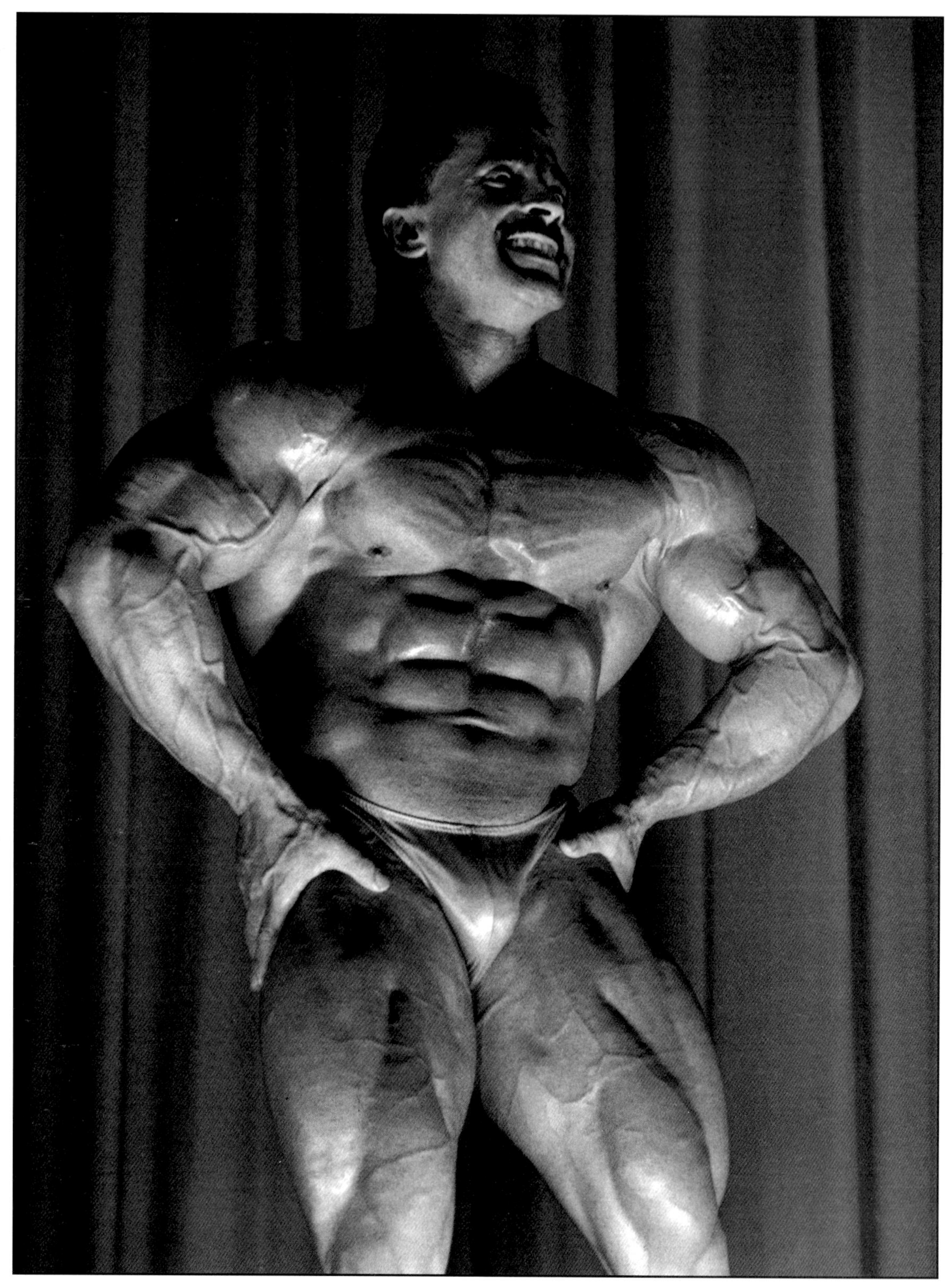

Samir Bannout, champion muscle man.

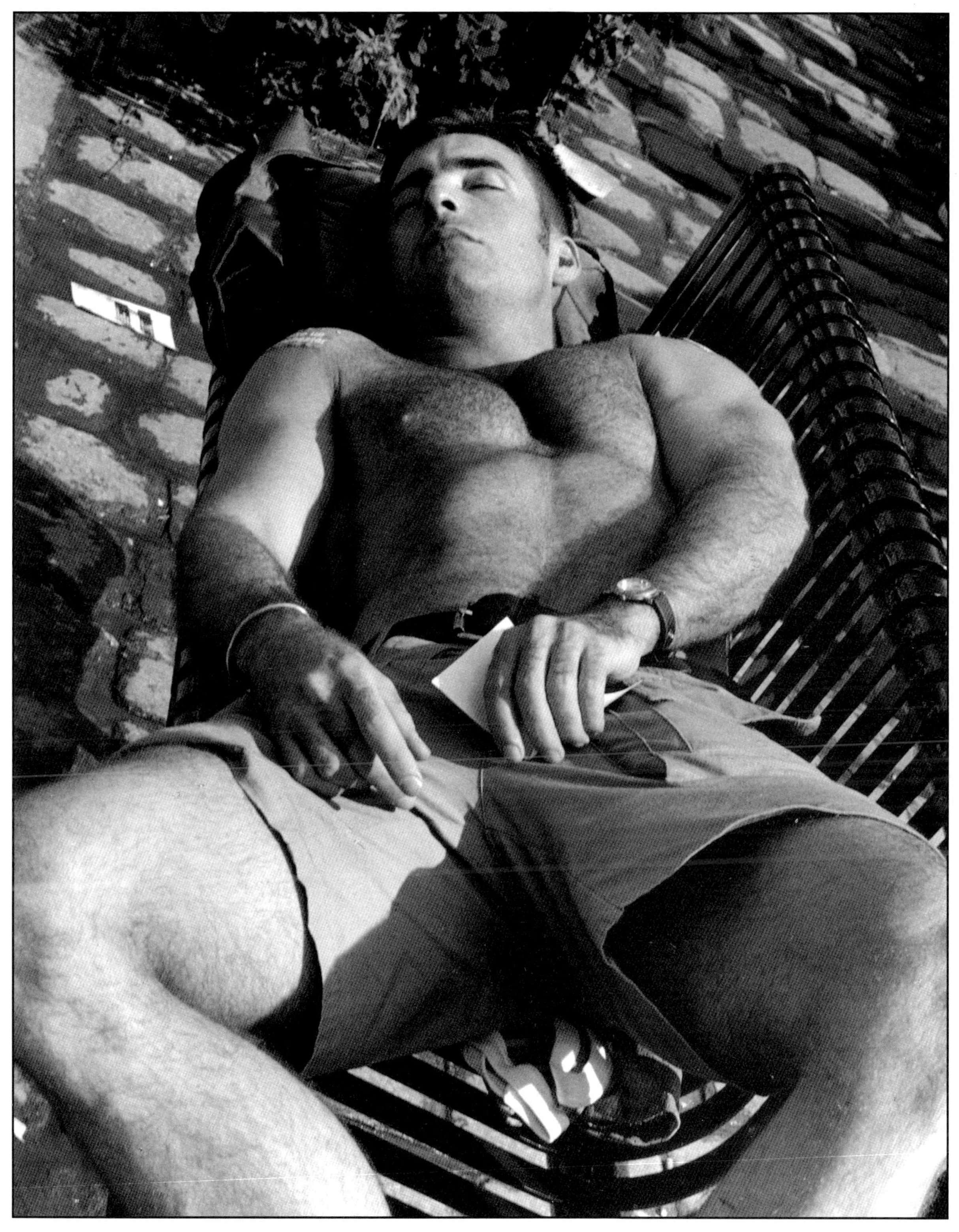

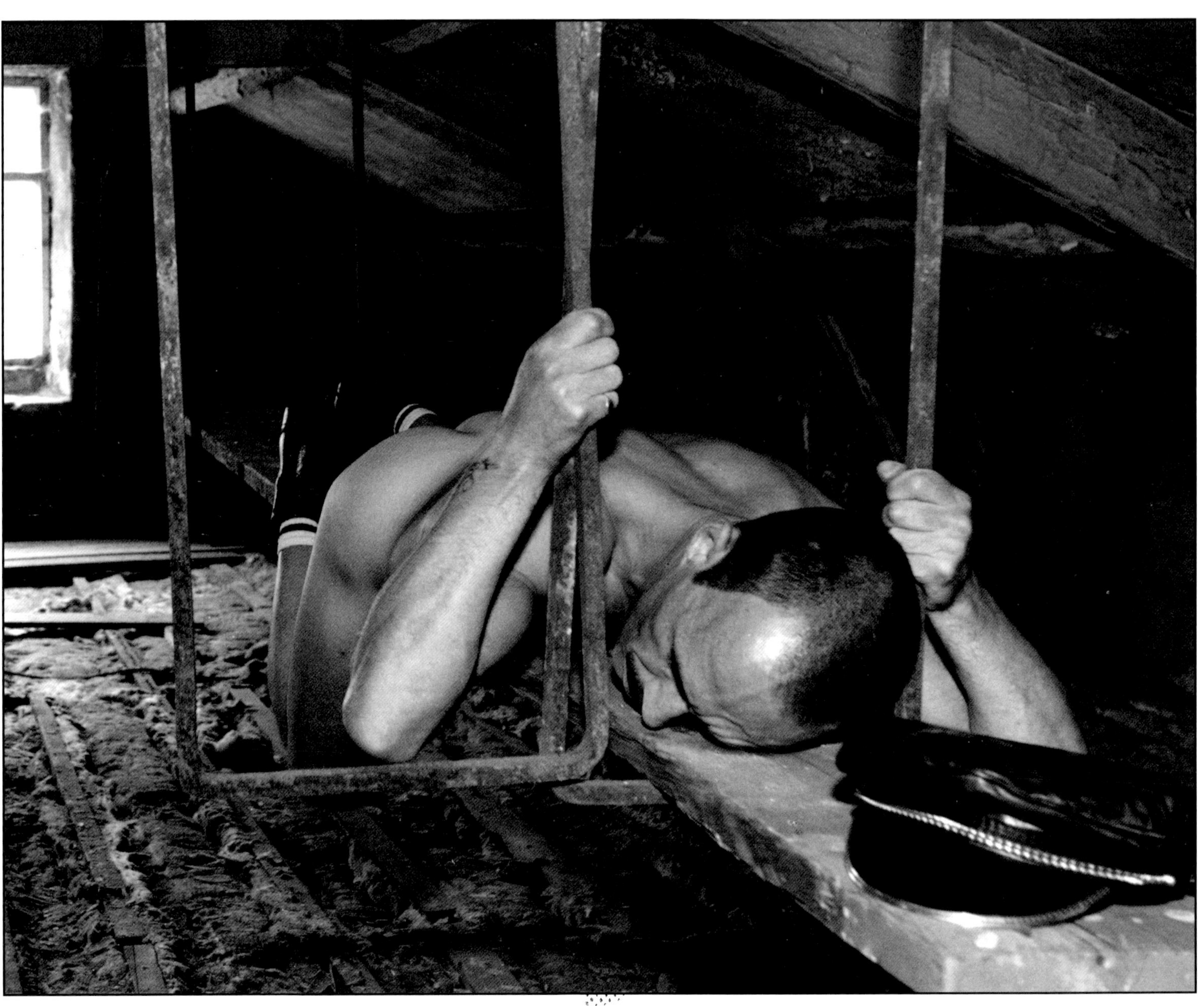

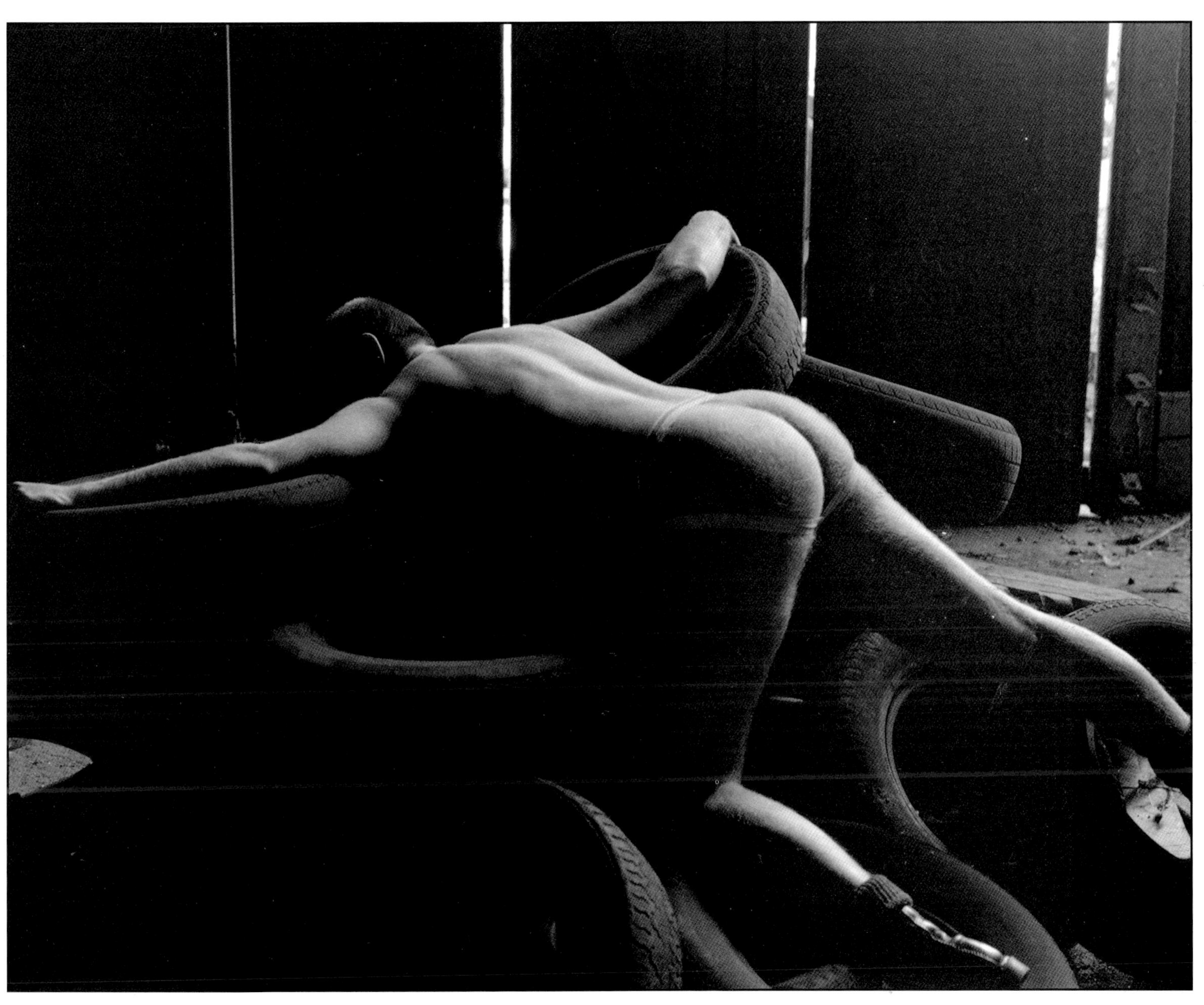

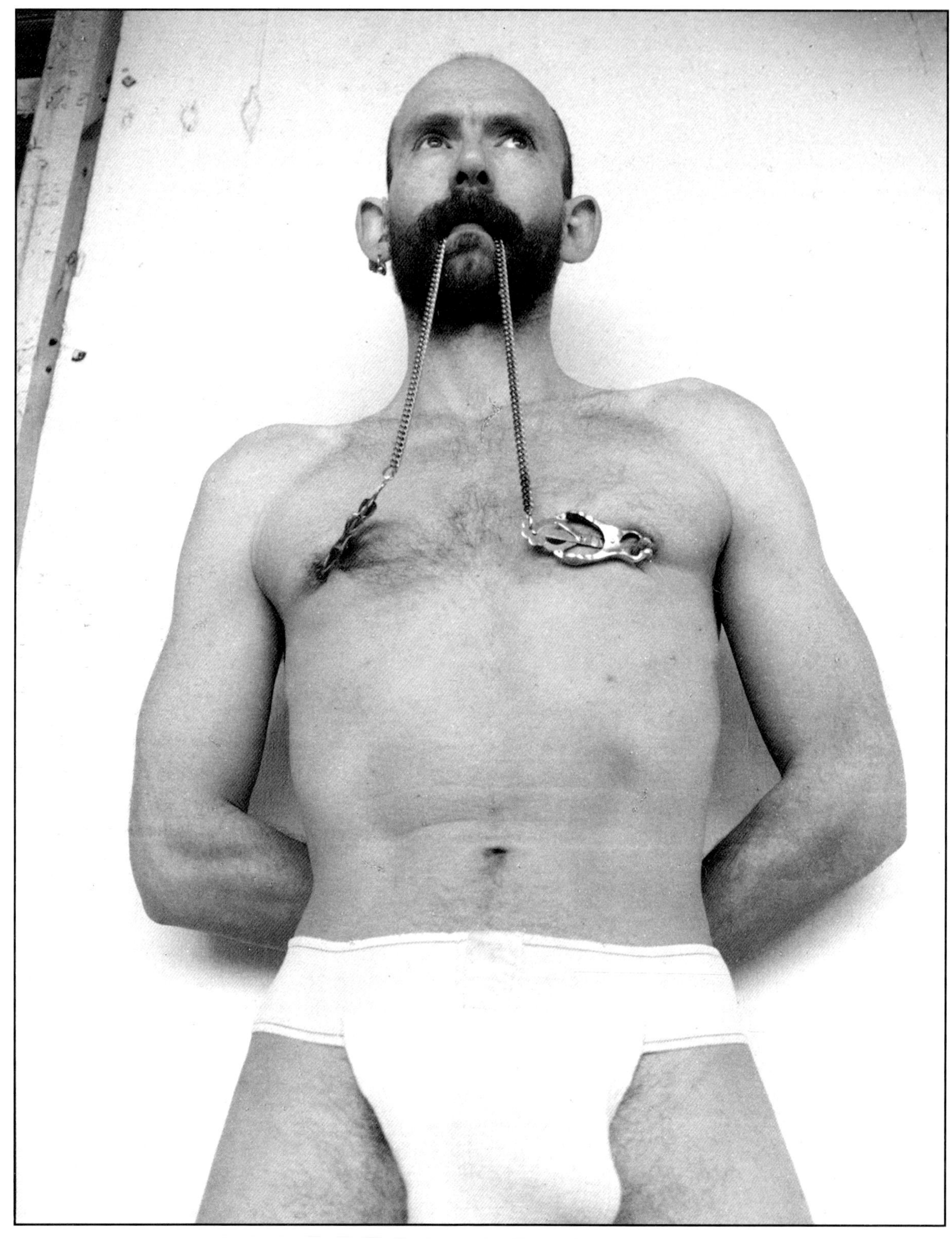

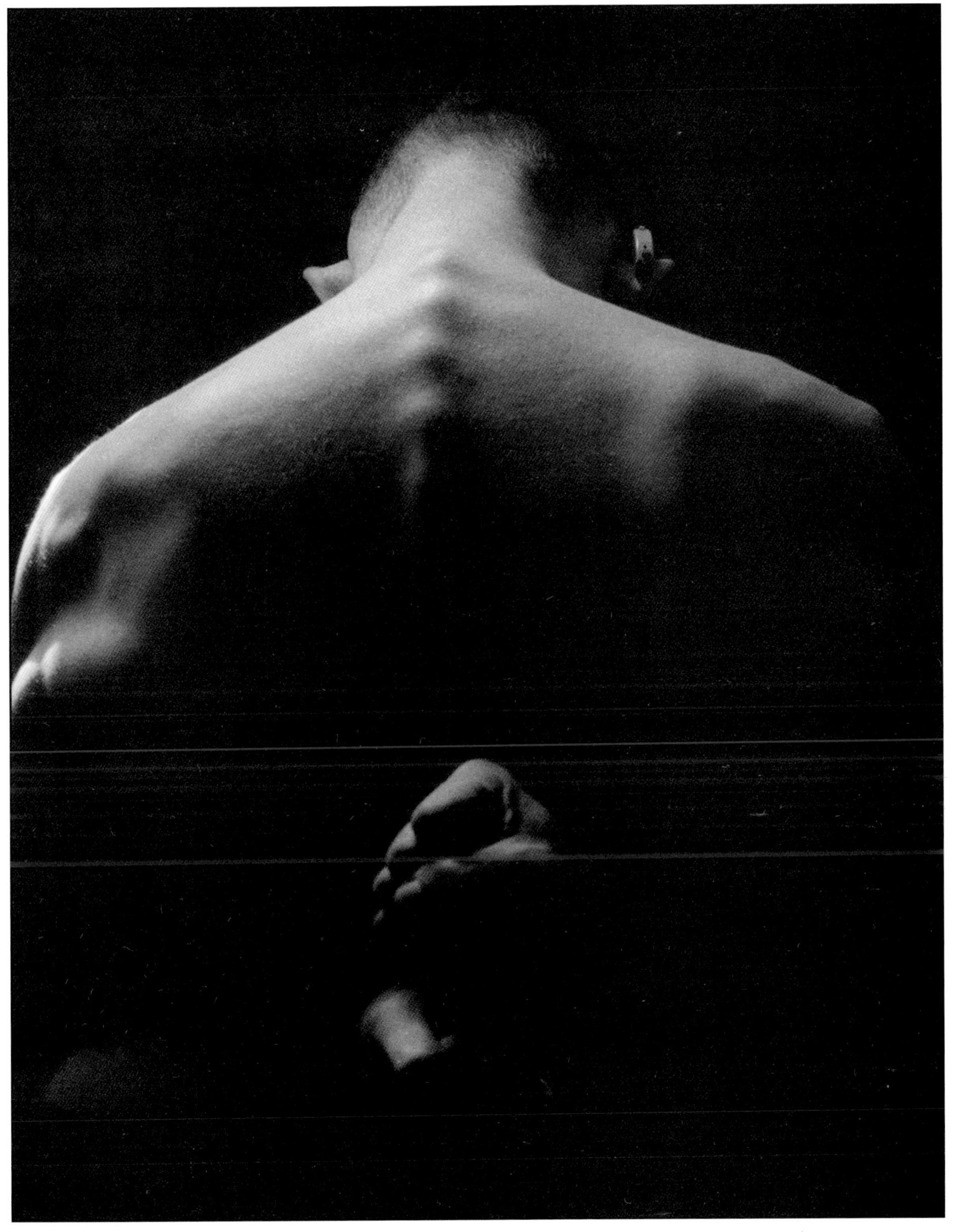

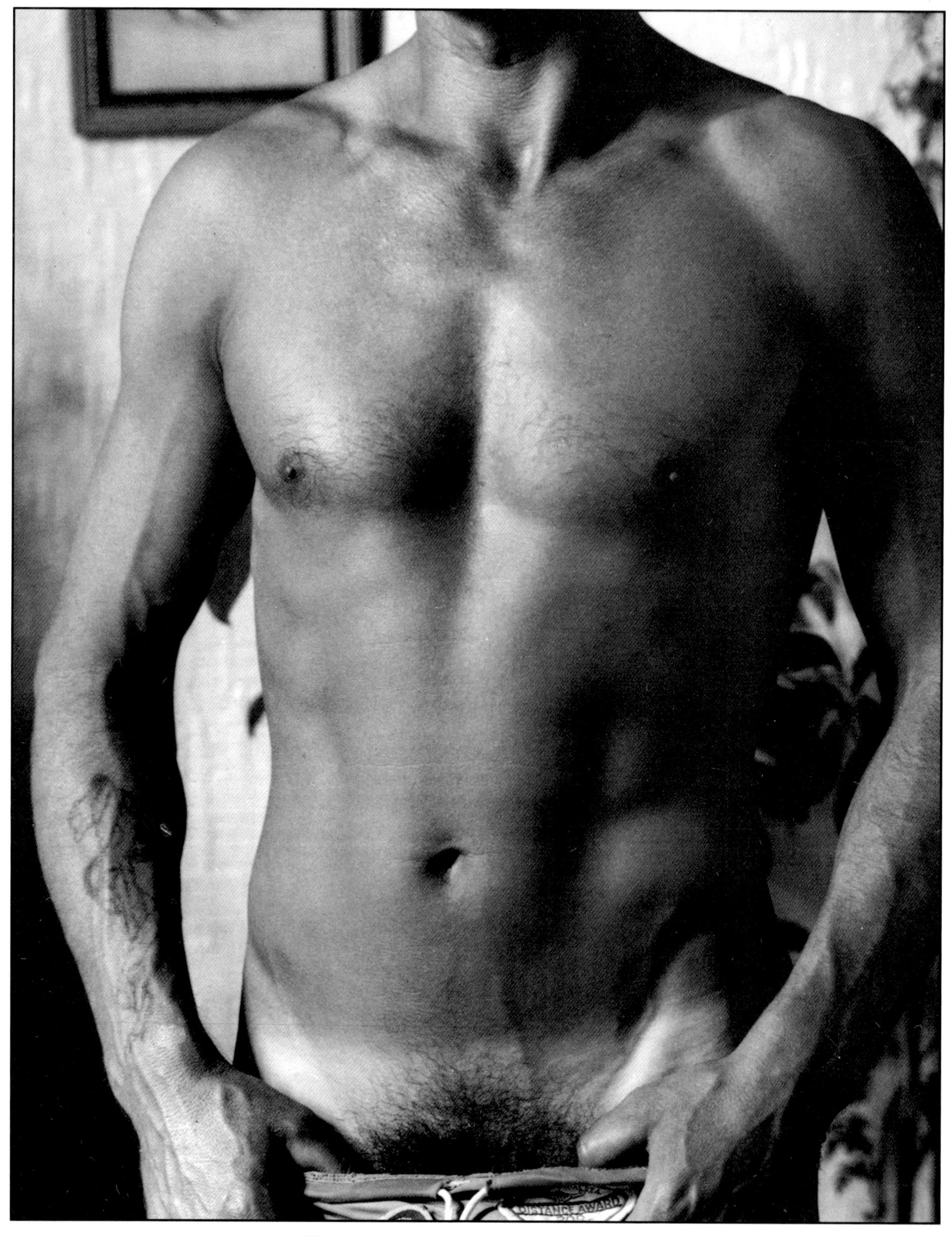

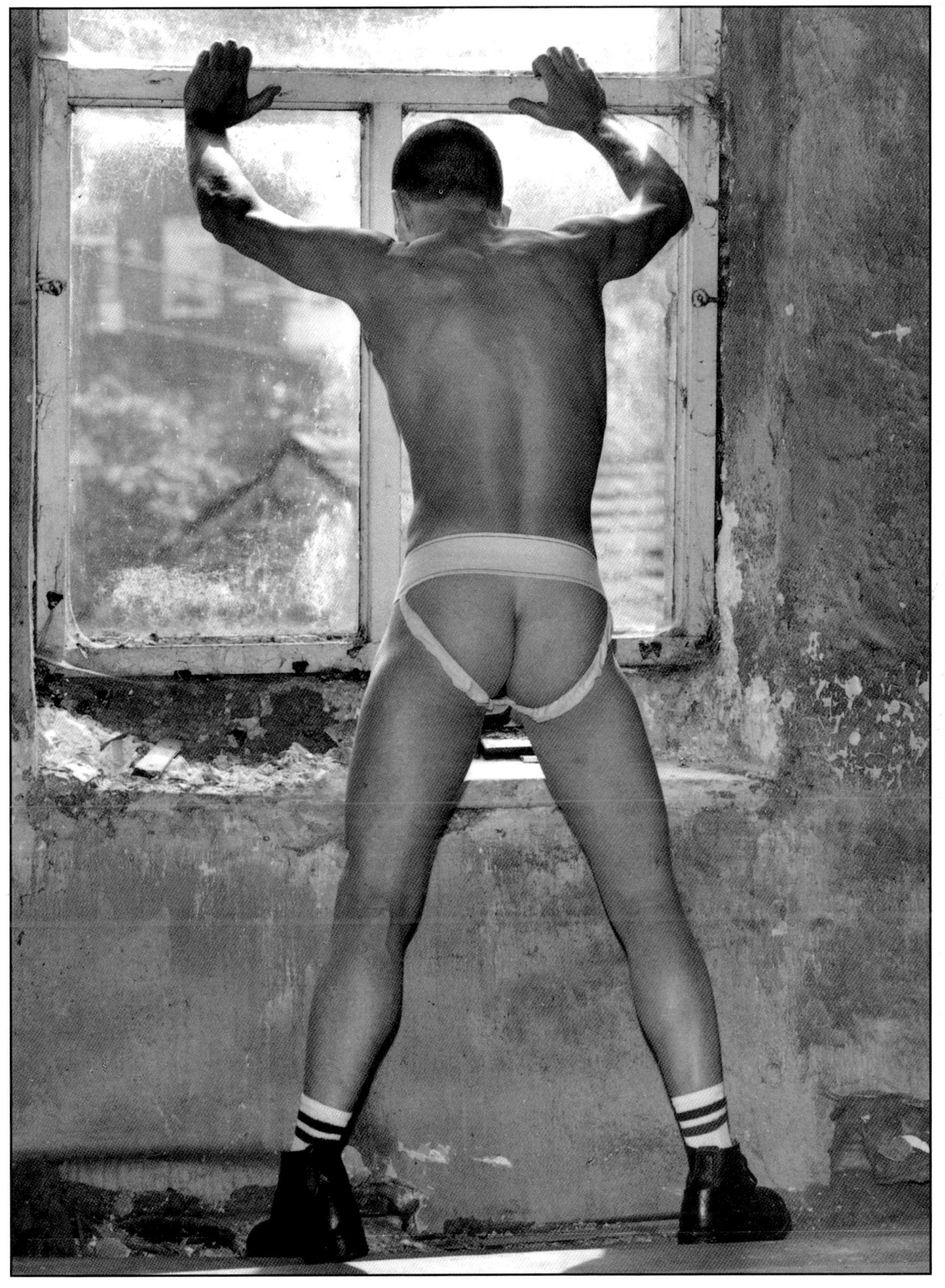

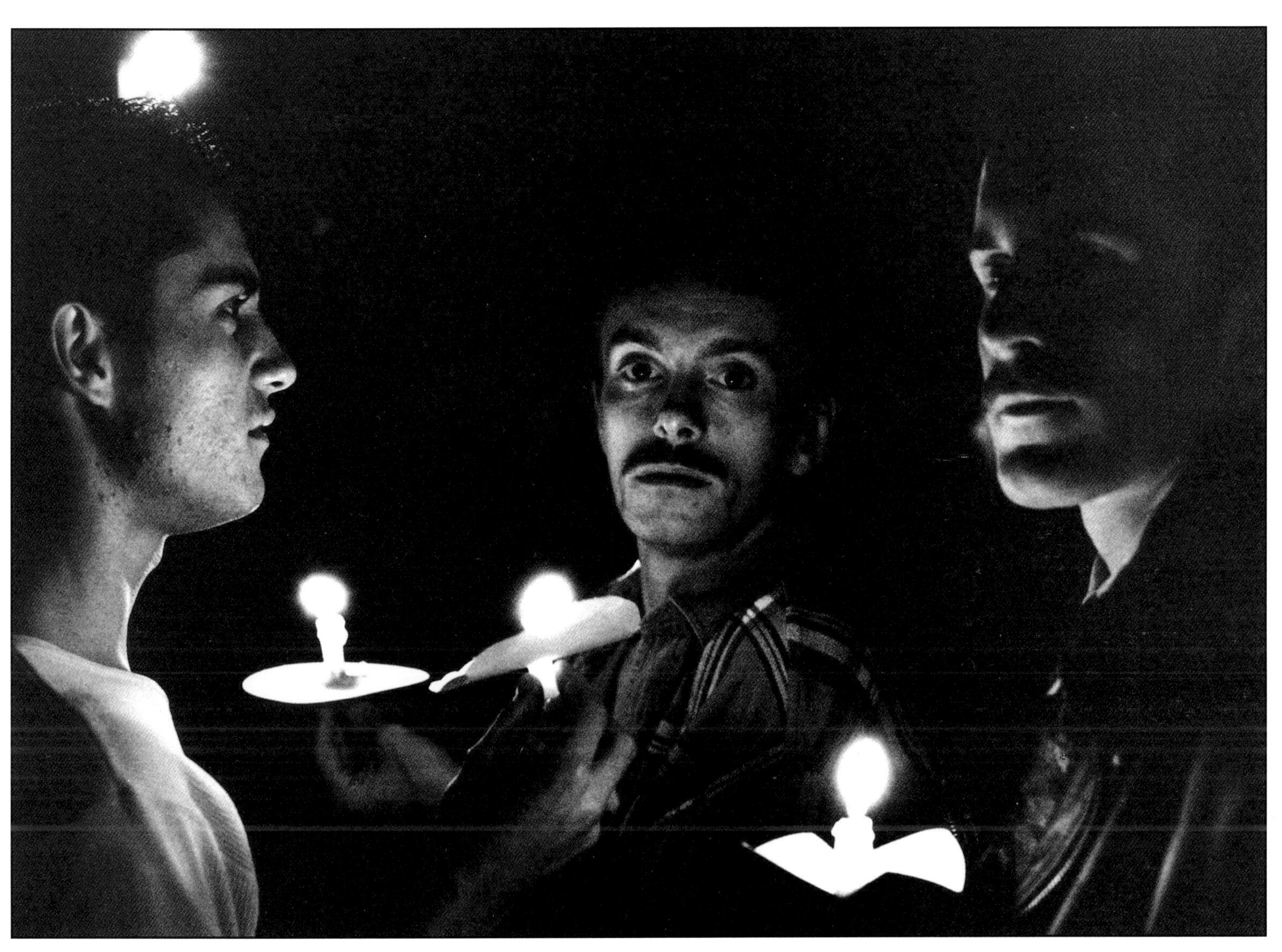